P7

LONDON BOROUGH OF BRENT
LIBRARY SERVICES

Harlesden Library, Craven Park Road, N.W.10
Tel: 965 7132

Please return this book by the date shown below. If it is kept
longer without renewal an overdue charge will be made. Books can
usually be renewed, unless requested elsewhere; if by telephone or
post, the book number and date due is needed.

All books are issued subject to the Bye-Laws and Regulations
approved by the Council, a copy of which may be seen at any Library.

23. OCT. 1976		
12. NOV. 1977		
27. NOV. 1978		
16. DEC. 1978		

The Lending Libraries are open 9 a.m. to 8 p.m.
(Wednesdays 1 p.m.   Saturdays 6 p.m.)

L & CO

Puppet Circus

By the same author

Introducing Puppetry
Punch and Judy

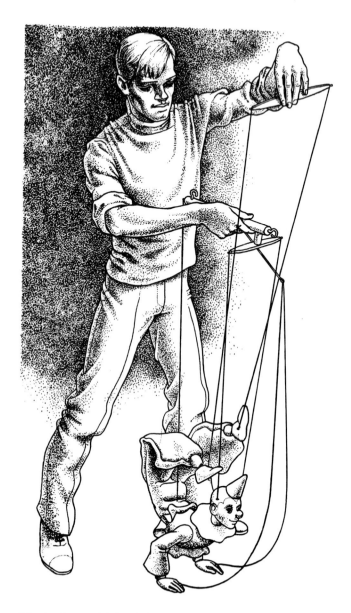

Manipulator with hand-balancing marionette

Puppet Circus

PETER FRASER

With illustrations by the author

B T Batsford Limited London

© *Peter Fraser 1971*
First published 1971
7134 2291 2

Filmset in Monophoto Baskerville, 11 on 12 pt
by Keyspools Limited, Golborne, Lancashire
Printed and bound in Great Britain by
C. Tinling & Co. Ltd, Prescot, Lancashire
for the publishers
B T Batsford Limited, 4 Fitzhardinge Street, London W 1

Contents

Introduction

In this book I have gathered together all the trick puppets I can find which may be used in a circus theme. For the puppet maker and performer, much of the pleasure and interest of these puppets will be found in overcoming problems of technique; for the audience there is always the question 'how is it done?' This is not a sphere of puppetry primarily concerned with story-telling or the expression of ideas, which might be thought the greater art. The scope of trick puppetry lies mostly in the vitality and ingenuity of movement for its own sake, and a circus setting displays this very well.

String puppets or marionettes provide the main traditional source of trick puppetry. This is not surprising as the marionette can give the illusion of moving independently of control; it can rise into the air and make use of whole body movement. Shadow and rod puppets are more limited, and glove puppets have little application here at all. Marionette theatres in this country have always been particularly strong in acrobatic techniques, and examples from the great Tiller and Barnard troupes of the later nineteenth century still survive. Although very different from the more subtle and expressive puppets of the Far East, they seem to me to be undoubted works of art.

9

Many of the puppets in this book are drawn from the late Victorian hey-day of the trick marionette. Unfortunately, written information on the subject is often incomplete, particularly in the description of controls, and in some cases I have had to simplify or invent, to find a working mechanism which is easy to explain and to make. However, I have tried them all out and they do work!

In construction and performance puppetry provides two fields of opportunity for educational aims or creative work. Not all people concerned with puppetry are equally interested in both, and some, perhaps, will find reward enough in the contriving of ingenious working toys without the extra involvement of presenting a show. However, in choosing puppets for a puppet circus, I have always kept an eventual performance in mind, and for those who are interested in combining many skills in a group performance I have included chapters on simple and quickly made puppets, and information on theatres and production.

A further section on working toys for children should extend the age group for which this book may be used. Strictly speaking, these are not puppets at all, but they do make a good introduction to the mechanisms used in shadow, rod and string puppets. Also, the making of jointed moving figures is a great help to young children whose representation of the human figure in paint or crayon often tends to be stilted.

With the older student in mind, I have designed my own puppets fairly close to nature. Young children are usually quite happy to work in the art room freely and without self-consciousness over inaccuracies of representation. In their case it would be a pity to interrupt the process. This freedom passes as students come to observe as well as to express; I hope that there is information here from which they may be able to develop their own stylisation or fantasy.

Simple working toys

Each of the following toys is chosen to show a particular type of leverage which can be developed for use with acrobatic puppets, particularly those worked from below. String puppets, worked from above have their own established tradition, but examples of shadow, rod and glove puppets are less easy to find. However, the mechanism of the jumping jack can be fitted to a great variety of shadow figures, and the jack-in-the-box puppet is the starting point of many combinations of rod and glove puppets. The leverage of the monkey on a stick is useful in both shadow and rod work, and the acrobats suggest further possibilities.

Most of these toys can be cut with scissors or a craft knife from cardboard, and jointed with carpet thread. With a little extra skill they may be cut in plywood using a minimum amount of tools—a fretsaw, hand drill, a small file, wire cutters and sand paper. Cotter pins and washers for wooden joints can be bought in a limited range of sizes, but they are easily made from wire bent into shape with round nosed pliers, the washers being cut from thin sheet tin or plastic.

Flat toys can be highly decorative as well as functional, and give plenty of opportunity for design. Practice figures are most successful when cut directly in card rather than drawn on paper, encouraging a natural sense of silhouette. When basic shapes are complete, details of costume can be added in paint or appliqué.

JUMPING JACK

The jumping jack is a flat toy with a very long history, and several types are known. I have described here a stringed jumping jack which hangs on a wooden bar held from above.

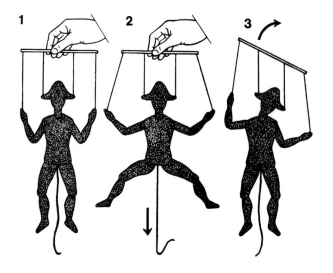

Figure 1
1 Here the jumping jack is in resting position. When not in use it can be hung on a hook making a good wall decoration.
2 When the string hanging below the figure is pulled, the legs and arms shoot outwards on either side.
3 Many extra movements can be carried out by tilting the top bar in different directions.

Figure 2   Jumping Jack

This toy can be cut in any size from 150 mm to 600 mm or more, using cardboard and carpet thread, or plywood with cord or cotter pins. Cardboard figures can be decorated in appliqué with coloured foil or fabric, while wooden figures, when sealed with grain filler and sandpapered, are painted with acrylic or poster paint.

Figure 3
Whatever the material used in making a jumping jack, a trial design cut in rough paper saves waste. Trial movements can be carried out by pinning parts on to a flat surface and rotating the limbs to see what movement takes place.

The joints of the jumping jack work on overlapping circles pierced through the centre. When the joint circles at shoulder and thigh are pulled inwards and down, the limbs below jump outwards.

Holes for jointing and stringing are pierced by a needle, leather punch, or hand drill, depending on the material from which the figure is made.

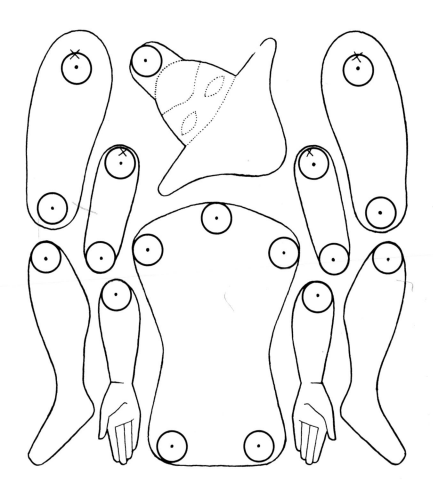

Figure 3 Parts of the Jumping Jack

Figure 4
A Cardboard figures can be jointed with thread which is knotted on one side, sewn through and glued under a cardboard disc on the other.

B Plywood parts may be linked by cord close knotted on either side, or more safely with cotter pins which hold metal washers between the wooden surfaces.

C Stringing is done in three parts; from side to side at shoulder and thigh joints, and in a vertical string which joins the two cross strings and hangs below the figure. The cross strings should be taut so that a slight tug on the hanging string causes movement.

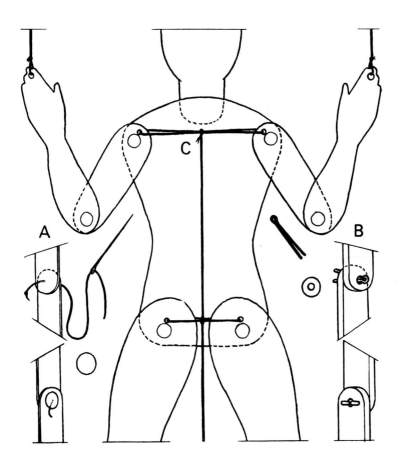

Figure 4   Jointing and stringing

17

The Jack-in-a-box puppet shows features of both rod and glove puppets. In the starting position the supporting stick is pulled downwards so that all of the lion's body is drawn into the box with the ends of the paws just appearing over the edge. When the rod is pushed upwards the lion jumps out of the box to the full extent allowed by the body material, and the arms spring sideways.

Figure 5   Jack-in-a-box

Figure 6

The framework of this toy is made from a 300 mm length of wooden dowel rod glued into a cotton reel, and a piece of cardboard 80 mm by 240 mm rolled into a cylinder. The pattern facing is redrawn on to 10 mm squared paper and traced on to material for the lion's head and body. The material should have some substance of its own. Felt or fur fabric are both suitable, and the pieces are cut out slightly larger than the pattern. When the head and body parts are pinned in position, wrong side outwards, stitching is carried out on the drawn line.

The three parts of the head are sewn, leaving the neck open, and the body is sewn up on each side. The head and body are turned right side out, and the head is firmly stuffed and glued on to the top half of the cotton reel. The body is glued at the neck on to the lower half of the reel joining the head, and the bottom edge is glued over the rim of the cylinder. When the ears have been sewn in place, the lion's mane, features, paws, and the box decoration can be completed with tufted wool, stitching, and appliqué material.

Figure 6   Pattern for Jack-in-a-box puppet

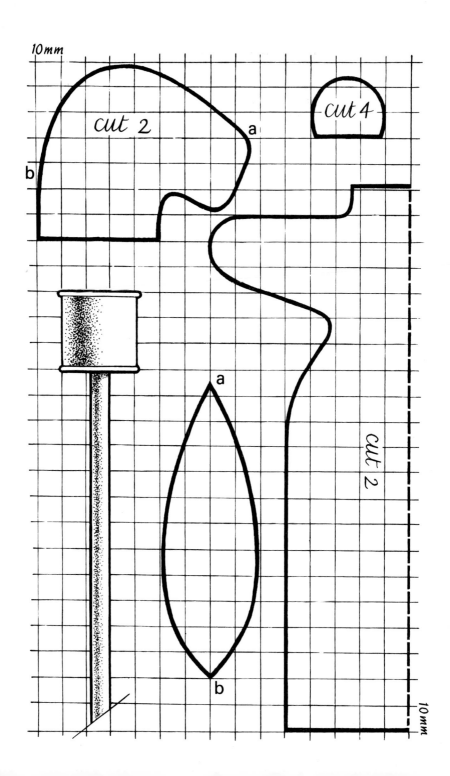

10mm

cut 2

b

a

cut 4

cut 2

a

b

10mm

MONKEY ON A STICK

Like the jumping jack, the monkey on a stick is a flat jointed toy of early origin which may be cut in carboard or wood. The figure moves on two wooden rods linked by a large screw eye or closed cup hook, one rod being slightly thicker than the other.

Figure 7   Monkey on a stick

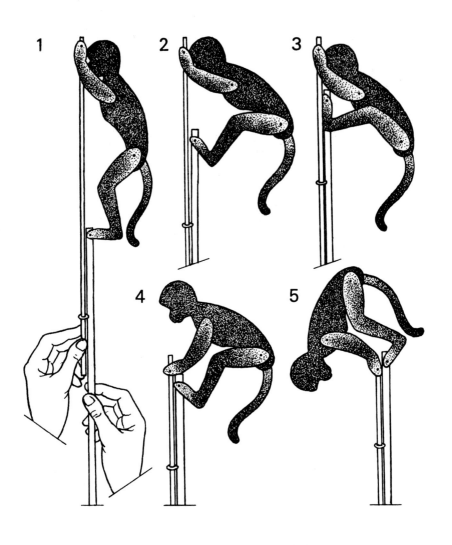

Figure 8
1   In the starting position the narrow rod is pushed upwards as far as the length of the monkey will allow, so that he appears to hang from a pole by his front paws.
2   The monkey's feet rise up the pole as the wider second rod is moved upwards beside the first.
3   The second rod reaches the level of the monkey's arms. The space between the arms is the same width as the narrow rod so the second rod cannot pass between them.
4   The wide rod pushes the monkey by the arms so that he swings over the top of the narrow rod.
5   The wide rod now appears as the pole which the monkey has climbed. As the narrow rod is lowered, he follows it down on the other side.

Figure 9

The parts of the monkey are cut in cardboard or plywood, and the two wooden dowel rods are drilled just below their top ends. The hands and feet are placed on either side of the rods, and like the shoulder and thigh joints are fixed with carpet thread, cord, or cotter pins and washers depending on the material from which the monkey's limbs are made. The tail moves on the same shaft as the thigh joint. This works very well with a cardboard figure, but is unsatisfactory in wood as the tail is easily broken and makes the distance between the legs too wide. The tail of a wooden monkey is better to be cut in PVC or thin metal.

Unlike the jumping jack, the monkey on a stick can be looked at from either side, and must be painted accordingly. The same principles on which this toy is made could be used equally well for an acrobat, or a lion.

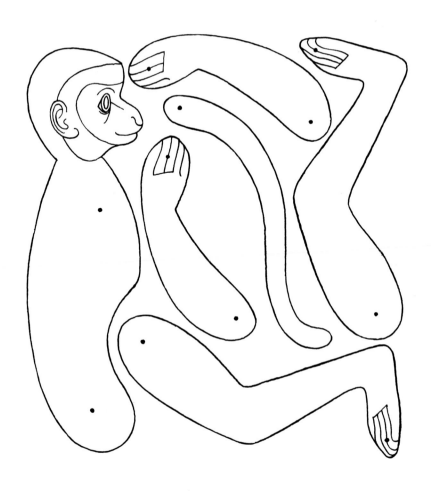

Figure 9   Parts of the monkey

Here are two circus roustabouts driving in a stake. The leverage which works these figures is very much like that of the monkey on a stick, but the parallel bars to which the figures are attached are horizontal instead of vertical. When the bars are level the tent raisers stand upright; when the upper bar slides backwards and forwards over the lower each figures strikes the post in turn.

The two tent raisers may be cut from cardboard in one flat piece and jointed with carpet thread to their cardboard levers *(see figure 10a)*. In this form they can be adapted directly for use as shadow puppets shown against a screen.

A more complicated toy is cut in separate plywood parts joined together to make three-dimensional figures *(see figure 10b)*. The body is cut in thicker plywood than the limbs, or built from two or three thicknesses of plywood glued together. The figures are assembled without movable jointing except where the legs and feet are attached by cotter pins to the bottom bars which are of the same thickness as the body parts. It is best to mark the position of the holes in the bar levers from each figure in turn in the striking position; when both figures are upright there is a slight gap between the bars. Although these solid wooden figures are cut in outline, the mallets and the post can be made from sections of dowelling, and a certain amount of rounding and modelling added to the figures with a file and sandpaper.

1

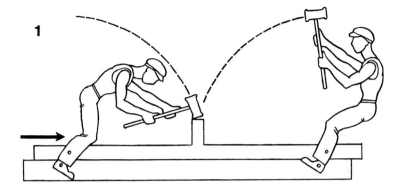

Figure 10a

2

Figure 10b

C

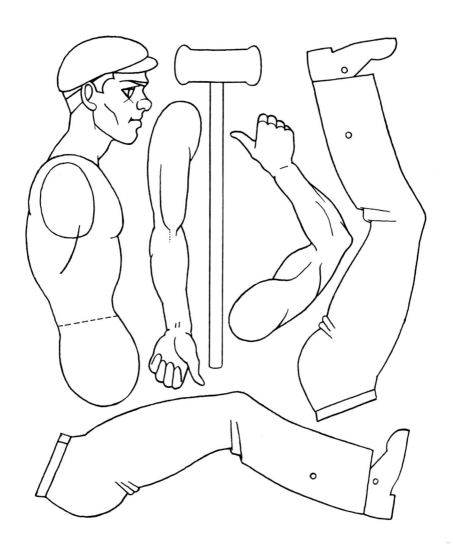

Figure 11   Parts of the tent raiser

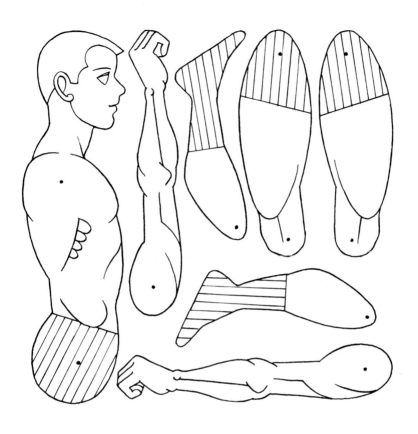

Figure 12　Parts of the acrobat

Figure 13 · *Acrobat*

The acrobat, like the tent raisers, is cut from separate ply-wood parts *(see figure 12, page 31)*, but here the limbs are freely moving, being jointed with cotter pins or cord knotted at each side. I have drawn a separate jointing for the knees as well as the shoulders and thighs, but the figure works equally well with the legs cut in one piece.

Figure 14 (overleaf)
There are two ways in which the acrobat may be made to swing over the bar. In the first (1) the figure hangs by the hands from strong twine between two upright posts. These posts are joined together below the acrobat's feet by a thick wooden crossbar and extend below it. The uprights are fixed to the crossbar by one strong nail on each side; no glue is used as some movement is necessary at this joint. When the ends of the uprights below the crossbar are pressed inwards the distance between the uprights above is increased, tautening the cord between them and pulling the acrobat round in a circle over the bar. The cord is threaded in a figure of eight (2) and the hands of this acrobat must be cut fairly wide if the movement is to be successful.

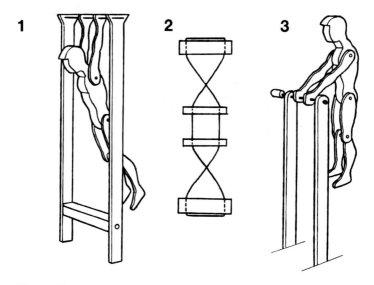

Figure 14

In a second type of movement (3) the acrobat hangs from a strong wire shaft between uprights which are glued as well as nailed to the crossbar below. The wire shaft moves freely in the holes drilled in the uprights, and is bedded into a short length of wooden dowel on one side. On the other it is bent with round nosed pliers into a loop so that it cannot slide out. The holes drilled in the acrobat's hands must be narrower than those drilled in the uprights so that the wire shaft can be tightly glued in place allowing no movement. When the dowel handle of the shaft is turned the acrobat raises himself by the hands and somersaults over the top of the bar. The handle can be turned backwards or forwards and at any speed causing the acrobat to move into many different positions. This toy makes a good basis for a rod puppet acrobat worked from below.

String puppets

STRING PUPPET CONSTRUCTION

Planning

Simple marionettes can be made from cloth; more elaborate string puppets may be directly modelled over a wire framework, cast in plaster moulds, or carved in wood. Sometimes two media are combined in one puppet as we see in the nineteenth century marionette which often had a lightweight cloth body with wooden head, arms and legs. Before beginning to make any puppet, a little previous planning is essential, and in a group activity a standard height must be set. Marionettes are usually from 450 mm to 900 mm high, but occasionally they are made as small as 300 mm, or as large as life size! Small puppets are easier to manipulate being light in weight, while larger puppets can be seen at a greater distance. The size of puppets therefore depends to some extent on the setting where they are to be shown.

String puppets are made in separate parts which are later jointed together, and it is most important to understand the relative size of each part to the whole. In the following diagram I have related the parts and joints of a wooden marionette to those of the human figure.

Figure 15

The head is usually taken as a unit of measurement with seven and a half units for the complete height. As you can see, the thigh joint is placed at half height, and the waist and elbow joints are level with each other. The shoulders are two units wide, and the hips one and a half units. The arm divides into three units from the mid-shoulder, and the length of the leg from knee to ground is two units. The hand is the same length as the face from hair-line to chin and the foot is one unit long. The female figure varies in that the shoulders and waist are narrower while the hips are wider, and the legs are proportionately shorter, altering the point of mid height.

The jointings of the puppet shown opposite allow most of the movement that we see in life, except that there is no sideways movement at the hip joint and very little at the waist, owing to difficulty in control. However, it is by no means necessary to aim for all these movements in every puppet that you make. Victorian marionettes seldom used a waist joint at all, and in the descriptions of the various trick puppets in this book it will easily be seen that each puppet is designed simply to carry out its own particular function. The extra mobility of excessive jointing is often a disadvantage. Neither is it absolutely necessary to follow the proportions shown above. Acrobatic marionettes are most easily handled if fairly small in size, (450 mm or less) and to extend the distance from which they can be seen, heads are often made a little larger than their correct proportion to the rest of the body, hands and feet.

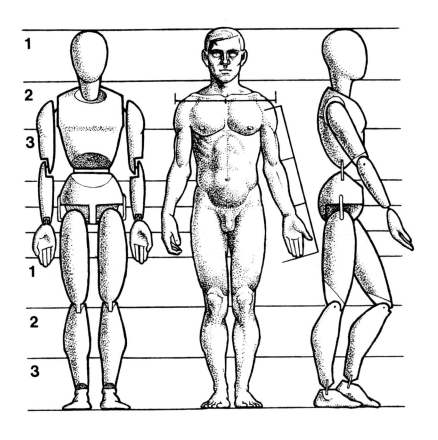

There are many ways of improvising cloth puppets. For those who prefer to follow a pattern, I have drawn one which can be copied on to 15 mm squared paper for a puppet 45 mm in height, or 20 mm squared paper for a 60 mm puppet. When the pattern has been traced on to material it should be cut with an extra width of 5 mm all round so that the stitching can follow the drawn line *(see figures 16 and 17)*.

The two parts of the body are sewn together round the edge, leaving openings at the neck, wrist and ankles. The body is then turned right side out and stuffed. Double rows of stitching at knee, elbow and thigh make good hinge joints, while the narrow spaces between the rows of stitching at the shoulders are tightly bound with thread to make freely moving joints. The head, hands and feet are most success-fully made in felt, and are turned inside out and stuffed in the same way as the body. They are then fitted over the neck, wrists and ankles and sewn or glued in place.

Ears, eyes and mouth may be completed in felt appliqué or paint; sometimes a papier mâché mask is fitted over the felt head. Hair can be stitched directly onto the head, and the divisions between the fingers of each hand are tightly sewn after the hands are stuffed.

Cloth marionettes, usually light in weight, are easier to control if small pieces of sheet lead are placed in the hands, above each knee joint, and at the base of the back for ballast.

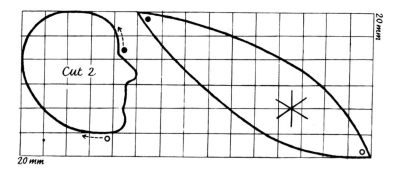

Cut 2

20 mm

20 mm

Figure 16

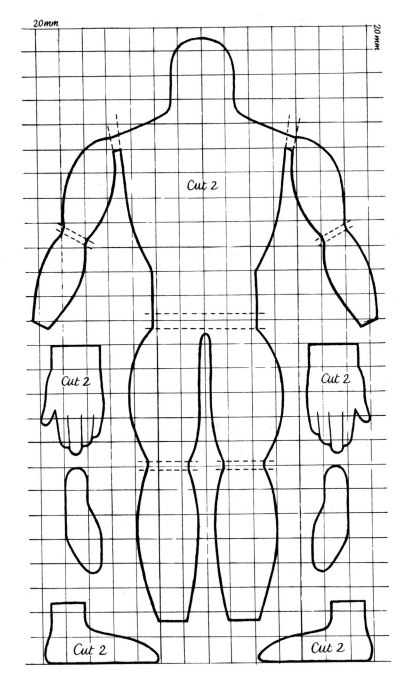

20mm

20 mm

Cut 2

Cut 2

Cut 2

Cut 2

Cut 2

Figure 17

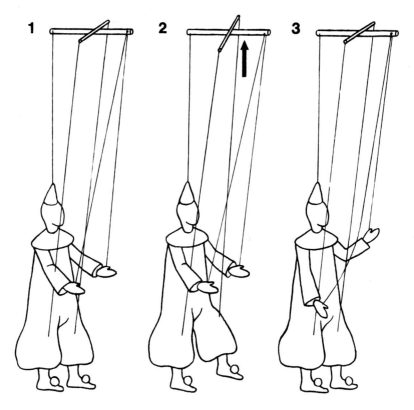

In spite of careful weighting, cloth puppets are difficult to control. They appear most successful when combined with rigid apparatus, (as the stilt walker and unicyclist), but the simple stringing described below is often used in puppetry with children.

Figure 18
1   One string to the head supports the clown's weight; strings from the cross bar are joined to each knee, and the hands are half raised on a running string through a hole in the main bar.
2   The main control bar is rocked from side to side for a walking movement.
3   The hands are raised or lowered by pulling on the running string.

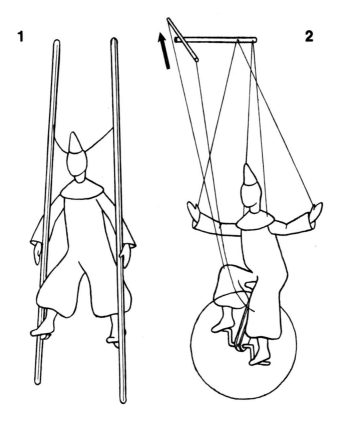

Figure 19

1 The hands and feet of the stilt walker are fixed to the stilts, while his head is supported on strings to each side. The manipulator's hands hold the stilts out of sight of the audience. This is a simple and most effective circus puppet, particularly when performing in a group.

2 The unicyclist is literally glued to his saddle, and his feet are fixed to the pedals of the wheel. The arms are raised on a running string through the main bar which rocks to raise and lower the knees. The shoulder strings support the main weight of this wobbly but convincing performer.

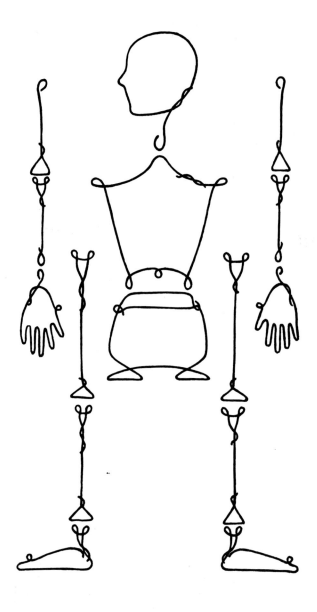

Figure 20

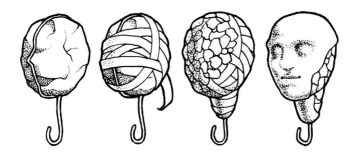

Figure 21

DIRECTLY MODELLED PUPPETS

The diagram opposite *(Figure 20)* shows a suggested wire framework for a directly modelled marionette. For convenience in copying I have drawn the parts separately, but before modelling begins the parts should all be interlocked, except for the head and hands which can be attached later. The drawings of the building up of the head *(see figure 21)*, show the method used for all parts of the body. The wire frame is either filled or surrounded with paper soaked in thin size or watered gum and the whole part bound tightly with bandaging. On this core the features and finished surface are built, using laminated and pulped papier mâché, or one of the plastic modelling substances described in the appendix at the end of this book. When this layer is dry it can be sand-papered smooth and sealed with spirit varnish ready for painting.

Screw eyes for string attachments can only be used safely with wooden puppets, so hooks for stringing must be included in the wire framework. When this has not been done, wire loops may be bedded with extra glue in the modelling material before it is dry. The hinge joints at knee and elbow are limited in range by the shape of the modelling; the joints at neck, shoulder and wrist are freely moving.

43

Figure 22

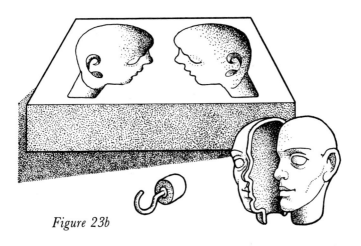

Figure 23a

Figure 23b

44

This may well be called an 'indirect modelling' method for making puppet heads, hands and feet. It can also be used for puppet bodies, but generally these are cut in soft wood which is light and easy to use for simple shapes. Of the many ways of making plaster moulds, the method described below is probably the easiest to control.

Parts to be cast are first modelled in plasticine, then eut with thin wire into sections without under-cuts. I find that the head is most easily cut into two pieces by a vertical section from back to front.

Figures 22 and 23a
The two plasticine halves are laid flat side down on a greased surface, and surrounded by a cardboard wall which is tied with cord and sealed by a roll of clay or plasticine. In this way a 'box' is formed ready to be filled with liquid plaster of paris.

A two pint jug holds sufficient plaster to make a mould of the two halves of the head. The amount of water needed can only be measured by eye, but it should be sufficient to fill the cardboard enclosure and to cover the plasticine halves by 20 mm. Plaster of paris powder is rapidly shaken into the water until it remains showing above the surface, and powder and water are sifted together by hand until the liquid begins to thicken. The mixture at this stage should be of the consistency of cream, and it is poured into the box in a steady flow until the plasticine halves are well covered. Within a few minutes the plaster begins to set, becoming quite warm in the process.

Figure 23b
After about 15 minutes the plaster mould should be firm enough for the removal of the cardboard surround. The mould is turned over, and the original plasticine half heads are carefully prised out. All the inside surface of the mould is cleaned with a paint brush and soap and water, and when the mould has been thoroughly dried in a warm place it is ready for use.

45

Press-mouldings or 'linings' can be taken from the inner surfaces of a plaster mould, using any plastic modelling substance which sets hard. Papier mâché has often been used for this process, but other suitable materials are described in an appendix at the end of this book. When the linings of the two halves of a head are dry, they are removed from their mould and glued together. Any spaces in the joining can be filled with the same material used for the linings. A large cup-hook screwed into a wooden cylinder is fitted into the neck, and the head is ready to be joined to the body *(see figure 23b)*.

Papier mâché pulp
is placed in pellets all over the inner surface of a mould which has been greased with vaseline. Firm pressure on the pellets welds the coat into one, about 5 mm thick, and the pulp lining should slightly overlap the edges of the mould to allow for shrinkage in drying. When the linings in each section of the mould are partly dry, the whole coating should again be pressed firmly with the thumbs to counteract shrinkage, and to re-define the shapes underneath. The overlapping rims of the pulp layers are now trimmed, and when dry, the separate linings can be removed from their mould and glued together.

Laminated papier mâché
is built up from several layers of fine absorbent paper in each section of a greased mould. When laminated papier mâché is nearly dry it is prised out carefully with a knife; unlike paper pulp it shrinks very little in drying. Press-mouldings from laminated papier mâché are thinner than those made from pulp, and when the separate sections are fitted together the inside of the joining must be strengthened with strips of bandage or paper pressed into place through an opening in the base of the neck.

Plastic wood
is placed in moulds in large flat pancake shapes, one to each section, and pressed into contact and trimmed at the edge

like pastry in a dish. There is no need to grease the mould
before using plastic wood. Instead, the whole plaster mould
is soaked in water before the plastic wood lining is applied.
Other modelling substances usually sell their own parting
agent, or need none at all when used with plaster of paris
moulds.

Choice of wood
Usually the head, hands and feet of a wooden puppet are
carved from hard wood (lime wood is perhaps best, but most
close-grained fruit woods can be used), while the parts of
the body can be cut from soft wood. If a puppet is to be
clothed from the neck to wrist and ankles, there is no reason
why circular sectioned wooden dowelling should not be used
in suitable thickness for arms and legs. Dowel limbs can also
be built up to shape with modelling substances after the
joints have been cut.

Tools
I find that for most purposes of carving, a 25 mm firmer
chisel for broad work and an 8 mm chisel for fine work do
very well. Other tools that you will need are a mallet, a small
needle file for finishing work and a saw or plane to shape
wood into rectangles ready for carving. Almost all of the
shaping of soft wood body parts can be done with an electric
sander if you have one. It is very important to keep wood
firmly in position while it is being carved. In the early stages
of work a table vice or G cramp is used. For finishing work
I usually hold the wood in a cloth in one hand, and use the
other to hand-pare with a chisel; or final work can be
screwed from below to another rectangle of wood which is
itself held in the vice.

Wood grain
An understanding of the grain direction of wood is essential
if you are going to carve successfully. In the standing figure
of a puppet the grain direction is vertical from top to bottom

except for the feet. Chisel cuts must always be made at an angle moving in the same direction as the grain. If this principle is forgotten, essential parts of your carving will split off.

CARVING

Unless you are an experienced carver, it is always safest first to make drawings of front and side profiles of all the parts of the puppet, and also a plasticine model of the head. In this way when you begin to cut the wood, you will know what shapes you are aiming for.

Wood is usually bought in rectangular sectioned lengths, although you may yourself have seasoned branch limbs which are circular in section. In either case it must be reduced by sawing or planing to rectangular blocks just over the height and width of the drawn profiles. The sample profiles which I have shown here *(see figures 24, 25 and 26)*, can be used as a guide for puppets made by direct modelling or from plaster moulds, as well as for puppets made in wood.

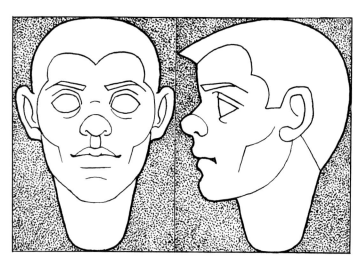

Figure 24   Profiles for wooden blocks
Figure 25   (opposite)

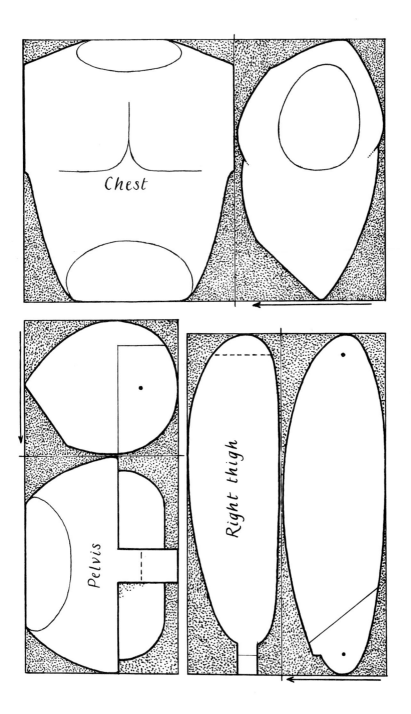

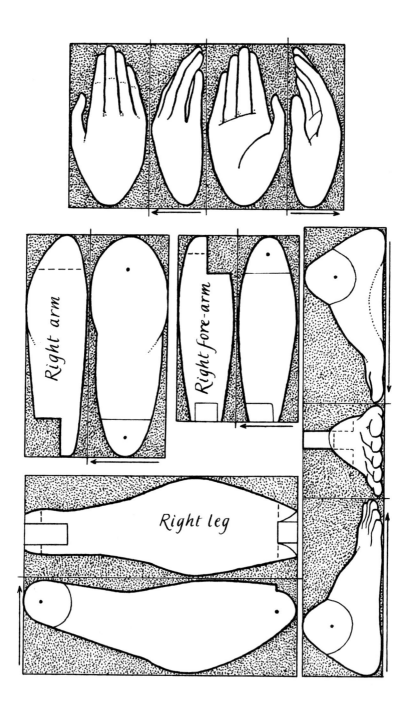

Figure 26   Profiles for wooden blocks (opposite)

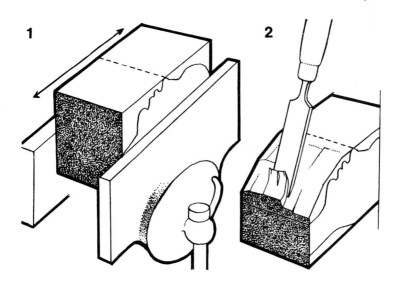

Carving a head

The stages of carving a head described here apply to all parts to be carved, although the head is the most difficult.

Figure 27a (above)

1 The head block, marked with its drawn profiles is placed in the vice face upwards. The grain direction of the wood runs from the top of the head to the base of the neck.

2 Two broad planes can now be cut using a mallet and wide chisel. The mallet should strike the shaft of the chisel in a series of sharp taps rather than with great blows. In this way there is more control over the chisel's direction, and less chance of dislodging the wood from its fixed position. The surface area from the line of the nose (the highest point) to the neck may be cleared first, and working in the opposite direction, the area from nose to forehead and top of the head.

3 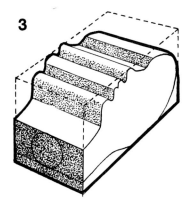   **4**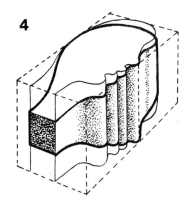

Figure 27b

3 All the angles of the features in profile are now chiselled out, turning the chisel round where necessary to follow the grain direction. The head can then be turned over in the vice, and the profile of the back of the head cut.

4 The head is turned sideways in the vice. To protect the nose and the back of the head, the block must be padded with folded rag where it comes in contact with the metal. The sides of the head from ear to neck in one direction and from ear to crown in the other are cleared.

Holding the head face upwards in the vice between the ears, the lines of the brows above the eyes leading to the bridge of the nose are cut out with a small chisel. The general shape of the eyeballs and mouth are defined, and the sides of the forehead and face rounded.

From this stage onwards the head may be screwed from below the neck to a block fixed in the vice, or held in a cloth in the hand. You may continue to work with a chisel or use a file to round the top and back of the head, cheeks, chin and neck. Hand paring carefully with a small chisel, details of eye sockets, mouth, nose and lastly ears are cut. The surface may be left with the chisel marks intact, or filed and sandpapered smooth.

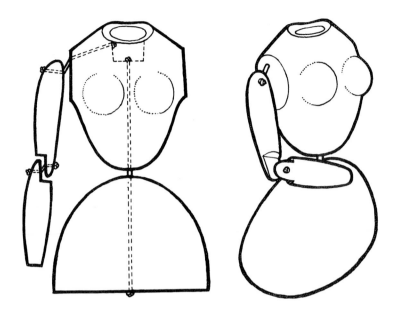

JOINTS

The joints of a puppet, whatever the material from which it is made, imitate where possible the joint movements of the human body. These may be either hinged joints as seen in the elbow, knee and ankle, or more freely rotating joints as at the neck, shoulder and wrist. There are three principal ways of jointing a wooden puppet—string joints, leather joints and tongue and groove joints. All three types may be combined in one puppet, and should be chosen with each individual function in mind.

String joints   *Figure 28*

String joints are the most flexible type of jointing, and are very useful where movement is to be sideways as well as forwards and backwards. A combined string jointing at shoulder and elbow makes for excellent arm movement with the ability to move across the front of the body. Sometimes a freely moving waist joint is made, using strong cord which can be continued upwards to make the neck joint.

Making a string joint for the elbow *Figure 29*

1 Two saw cuts remove a little over half of each end to be jointed. When the two ends are fitted together there should be a narrow vertical space left between them.

2 A hole is drilled through the centre of each projecting tongue at the joint ends.

3 The projecting tongues at the joint ends are filed or sand-papered round.

4 String or cord is passed through the drilled holes from one side to the other of the joint. Inside the joint the space between the tongues is loosely strung, and the outside ends of the string are knotted, cut close and painted with glue for safety.

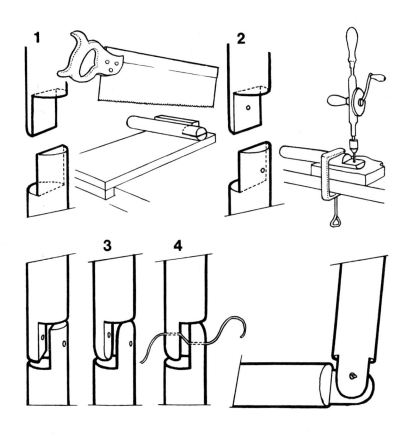

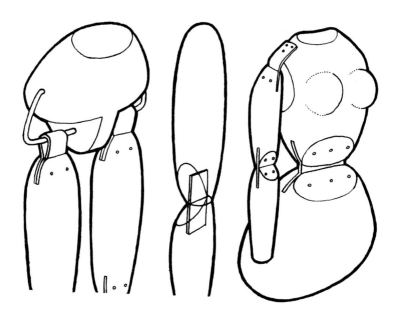

Leather joints   Figure 30
Leather joints make a very good hinge where movement is
forwards and backwards only. Good examples of this are
the knee, elbow and ankle joints. A leather joint may also
be used at the shoulder and at the waist if no great sideways
movement is needed. Leather used must be strong and
supple. For small puppets chamois leather is sufficient, but
for larger puppets men's gloving leather is best, or even
book-binders' morocco.

Making a leather joint for the knee   Figure 31 (opposite)
1   A straight saw cut is made down the centre of each part
to be jointed. These saw cuts should be exactly opposite
each other, and the cuts of the same width as the leather to
be used.

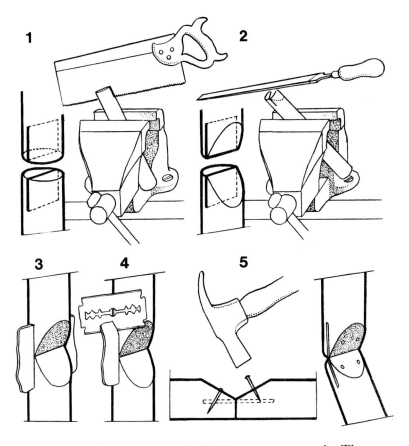

2   One half of each joint end is filed or cut to an angle. The degree of the angle controls the range of movement in the finished joint.

3   A square cut piece of leather is eased into each groove in turn, until the ends of the joint fit closely together. A little glue is run into the bottom of each groove, but kept free from the joint ends.

4   The overlapping leather is trimmed with a razor blade close to the sides of the joint.

5   After testing movement to see that the joint is not too tight, two small pins are tapped into each filed surface of the joint to pierce and fix the leather.

Tongue and groove joints

Tongue and groove joints are the most difficult to make. However, they give a more natural appearance than any other type of jointing and are particularly useful with acrobatic puppets where knee, elbow and ankle joints may be exposed. Tongue and groove joints are often 'stopped' on one side so that movement can be in one direction only from an extended position; for instance in the bending of knee or elbow joint.

Making a tongue and groove joint   Figure 32

1   Two vertical saw cuts in the end of each part to be jointed are made opposite each other, dividing the end surfaces into equal sections. In the upper part two further side cuts remove each outer third, leaving a projecting tongue, and shoulders lying at an angle. The angle of the shoulders controls the range of movement in the finished joint.

2   The lower part to be jointed has its centre third chiselled out at an angle as shown. The chisel used should be of the same width as the groove to be cut.

3   A small notch is cut from the short side of the tongue, and the groove in the lower part of the joint is deepened and notched to allow the tongue to fit.

4   The end of the tongue is filed round, and the surfaces of the lower half of the joint are also rounded.

5   The tongue and groove are fitted into each other, and drilled through from side to side. The size of the drill bit should be the same as the wire to be used in fixing the axis of the joint.

6   A short length of wire is passed through the joint, and cut short and turned over at each side.

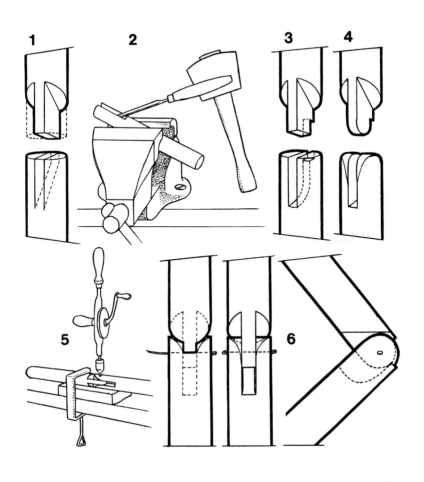

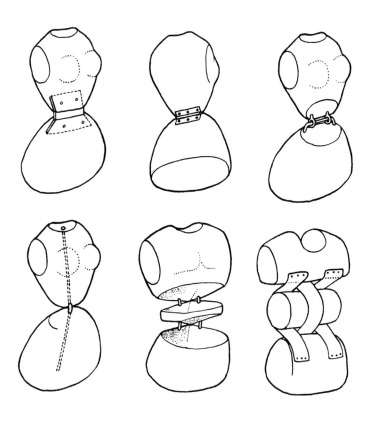

Irregular joints   Figure 33

Instructions on the making of string, leather and tongue and groove joints can be applied directly to knee and elbow joints. Other joints, although made by similar methods, need a little extra description.

Above are shown various types of waist joint, each with its own particular range of movement. Two are leather and two are string-jointed while a fifth uses a small metal hinge. The joint formed by two screw eyes on a wire shaft fixed into holes drilled in the wooden pelvis is perhaps the most commonly used of all.

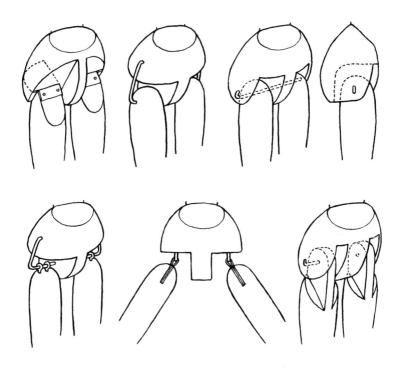

Figure 34
Thigh joints may be as varied as waist joints in construction
and range of movement, and should be chosen with the
function of each individual puppet in mind. Some have
complete forward and backward movement, while in others
the range is deliberately limited. Except in the case of some
dancing puppets, sideways movement at the thigh joint is
usually avoided as it makes walking very difficult to control.

61

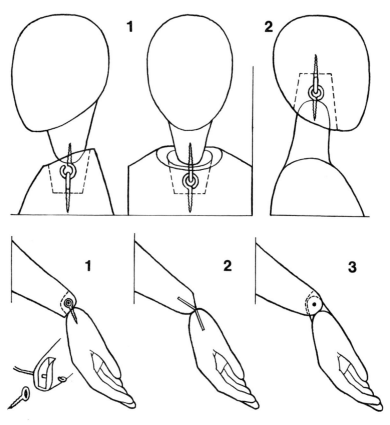

Figure 35

Here are two types of neck joint. In the first, two cup-hooks are screwed into the neck and the socket below. When interlocked they allow forwards, backwards and sideways movement. The second type of neck joint is concealed within the head but has less range of movement.

In the three types of wrist joint the first is formed by a screw-eye on a wire shaft allowing some sideways movement, while the leather and tongue and groove joints are straight hinges. Except in the case of hand balancing puppets the palm usually faces forward with the controlling string attached to the outer thumb side.

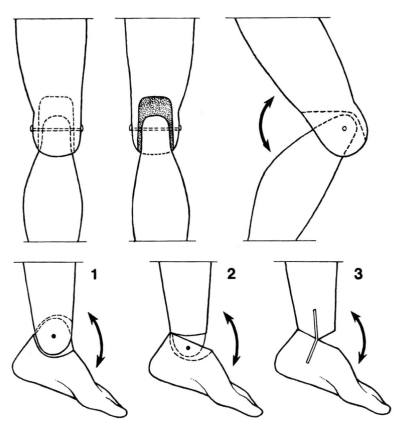

Figure 36

The concealed knee joint above is useful for acrobatic puppets with exposed arms and legs. The same joint may also be used at the elbow. Sometimes, if thick wire is used for the joint shaft, the ends can be divided with a narrow file and the two tongues turned over.

Ankle joints should be cut with the feet pointing slightly outwards to avoid tripping. Two types of tongue and groove joint are shown here and also a leather joint. The extent to which the foot may drop, sometimes controlled by stringing, is more simply limited by the shape of the joint itself in acrobatic puppets.

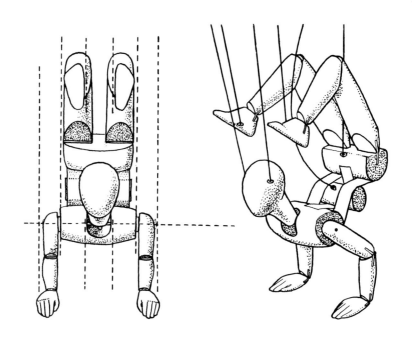

Movement in one plane   Figure 37

Some puppets are designed to move in one plane only, and
the contortionist, hand balancer and trapeze acrobat are all
made in this way. The drawing above shows how all the
joints except for the shoulders and neck are leather hinge
joints allowing no sideways movement. The shoulders rotate
freely on a stout wire shaft which is glued in place where it
passes through the chest piece. A narrow washer is fitted on
either side of each shoulder, and the wire ends are divided
with a small file into two tongues which are bent over. The
hook at the base of the puppet's neck can be fixed round the
wire shaft where it passes through the neck socket. This same
method of jointing is often used for the legs of animals.

1 Support of the puppet
The main weight of the standing puppet is nearly always carried by the shoulder strings. Head strings may take the whole weight of very simple puppets, but usually they support and move the head alone. A string to the puppet's back also supports weight in some positions and combines with the shoulder strings to balance the figure and keep it steady. These five strings are fixed permanently to a main control bar—sometimes known as the crutch or perch—which is held in the manipulator's 'supporting' hand.

2 Movements resulting from the position of the main control bar
In most puppet controls the tilting forward of the main bar makes the puppet bow, and sideways tilting alters the position of the head. Jumping, knee bending and lying down all result from the raising and lowering of the crutch, while the performance of some trick marionettes relies entirely on a 'tip up' control in which the whole main bar is reversed.

3 Individual movements carried out by detachable bars, wire levers and running strings
Although described and used separately, extra bars, when not in use, are hung from hooks on the main bar. The most common of these bars is the hand bar, worked by the operator's 'free' hand, with a string from each end running to the thumb side of each of the puppet's hands. Many manipulators use a separate leg bar, although this may be permanently fixed as a swivel bar to the main control and worked by the thumb of the operator's 'supporting' hand. Wire levers which raise and lower the puppet's hands are sometimes attached to the main control. Some operators thread the puppet's hands on a running string which passes freely through a screw eye on the main control bar.

Puppet controls can be made from broom handle, wooden dowelling, and cut plywood shapes to suit the demands of each puppet. All of the mechanisms described above can be seen working in different ways in the marionettes of the puppet circus.

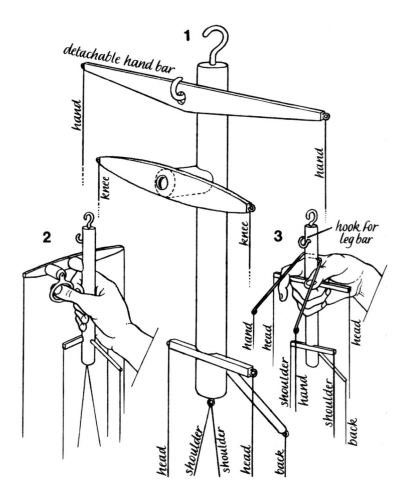

Three types of vertical control   Figure 38
1   A typical vertical control which is half the height of its
puppet. The swivel leg bar is worked by forward projecting
fingers of the supporting hand.
2   The same control is shown with a thumb attachment to
the leg bar.
3   This control has a detachable leg bar and wire levers for
the hand strings.

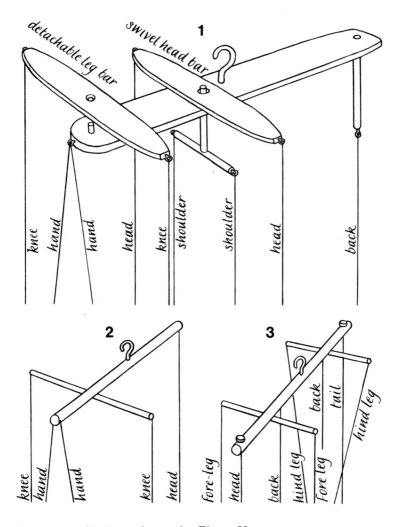

Three types of horizontal control   Figure 39
1   A standard horizontal control with a detachable leg bar.
2   A simplified horizontal control. Alternate side to side rocking raises the knees in turn.
3   A simple animal control bar. The strings to the hind legs cross over so that each is raised with the front leg on the opposite side.

Tip-up controls

Two kinds of tip-up control are often seen in trick puppetry. In the first the control bar, which has a vertical starting position, is imitated in all its movements by the puppet below; when the bar is reversed, the puppet, by means of heel and back strings, is reversed as well. In a second type, the main support to the puppet remains constant at head or shoulders, but the forward tilt of the control slackens and releases secondary strings.

An example of the first type can be seen in the contortionist acrobat. The puppet has a freely flexible waist joint, and except at the neck is hinged throughout to move in one plane only. The control bar is exactly two thirds of the height of the contortionist, and there are six main strings. Two are attached to the head, two to screw-eyes in the insteps of the feet, and there are two backstrings, one taut to the centre piece of the waist joint, and one slack to the base of the pelvis. The cross strut for foot strings is wider than the strut for the headstrings.

Figures 40a

1 Here the contortionist stands upright supported by the head-strings. One back string is taut, while the other hangs loose.

2 As the control bar is tipped forward the puppet moves onto his knees, and the arms (weighted at the hands) swing forward. When the bar is horizontal, he rests on the ground with raised heels and head.

1

2

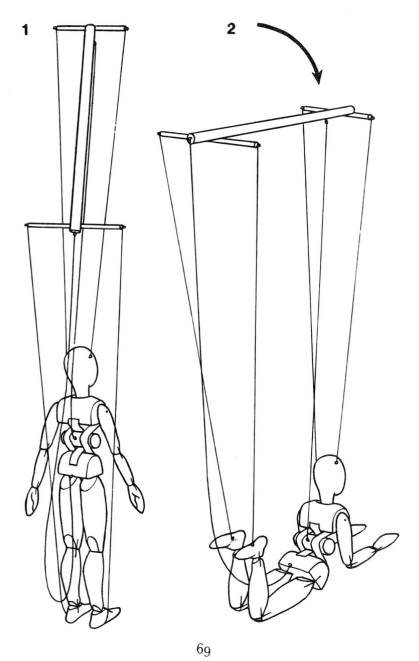

Figure 40b

3 The end of the control bar supporting the head remains in position, while the opposite end is raised vertically, drawing the heels upwards. The back string to the pelvis becomes taut (its length is measured for this position) taking over from the waist string which slackens. If the joint angles at wrist and elbow are correctly cut, the contortionist should now balance steadily on his hands.

4 The head string end of the control bar is now pushed backwards between the heel strings, drawing the taut backstring with it. The heel string cross bar moves forward, lowering the puppet's heels to his shoulders.

3

4

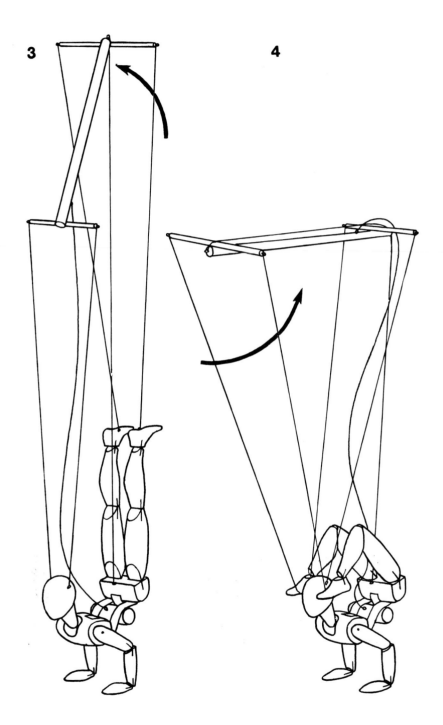

Figure 41
A second type of tip-up control is seen in this collapsing puppet. The upright position of the bar keeps the arms and legs in place by means of running strings through a screw-eye at each shoulder, and a hole at each side of the hips. Walking is controlled by a detachable bar moving arms and legs together, and the head may be raised and lowered on its own.

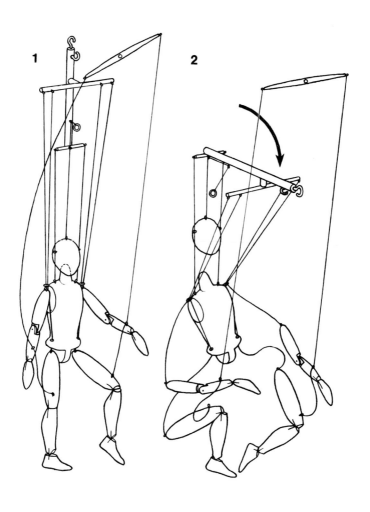

Tandem controls   Figure 42

Tandem controls are particularly useful when animal (or human) puppets are performing in groups—two or more puppets on one control can be handled by a single manipulator. The control shown below is merely an extension of the standard horizontal control bar which rocks from side to side to cause a walking or trotting movement. The main bar supports the weight of the puppet while the side struts alternately raise and lower the knees. This control may be used for numbers of any type of animal or human puppet arranged in single file.

Animal puppets can be made by any of the methods described for human puppets, starting with a drawn plan *(see
figure 43 below)*. Unfortunately when they are made in
proportion to the other performers in the puppet circus,
animal puppets tend to be rather heavy. This can partly be
overcome by the use of balsa wood for the main simple body
shape, but an animal as large as the elephant must be
modelled over a wire frame.

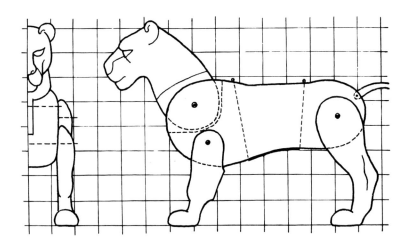

Figure 44

Although animal heads can be carved, modelled, or cast, the simplest method is to glue two linings from a mould to either side of a cut plywood profile which includes the tongue of the neck joint (1).

Legs can be cut in profile from flat sections of hard wood using a spring-saw or fret-saw, then filed or sand-papered to shape. The balsa wood body can be shaped entirely by sanding, and the neck groove cut out with a razor blade and sharp chisel (2).

Wire shafts for the leg joints pass through the animal's body and are glued in place. The legs rotate freely on the ends of these shafts, and are fixed with a small washer on each side. Wire loops for the body strings must pass right through the balsa wood and support the weight from underneath. Animal tails can be made of cord, or from felt or leather over a wire stiffening.

The tongue and groove joint, often used for the neck, allows no sideways movement. For some animals a ball and socket string joint is a useful alternative (3).

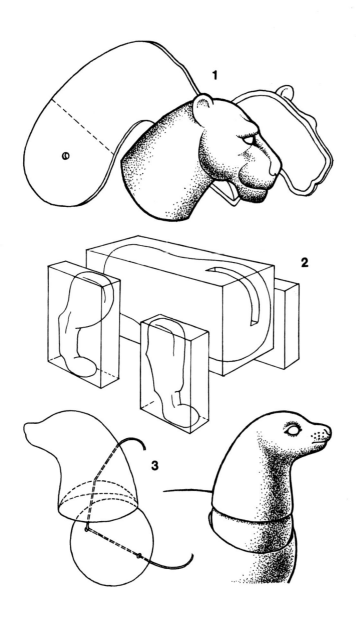

Animal controls   Figure 45
1   This control bar has supporting strings only. Forward and backward rocking of the bar causes a bounding or cantering movement. The leather flippers of the seal, hinged on wire staples, move freely with the body.
2   In a second type of control, side to side rocking raises the legs alternately. The cross-over strings to the back legs (described in detail with the circus horse) make the leg movement sequence correct for all animals except the elephant where they are not necessary.

The heads of both seal and lion are supported by strings from a wooden knob at the end of a spring or length of elastic attached to the main control.

1   **2**

Figure 46

A second type of tandem control supports animals arranged side by side, and the forward and backward rocking of this control brings about a bounding or galloping movement. In the example shown below two supporting strings are fixed to the back of each performing seal, while an extra detachable bar moves their heads and guides a ball which they throw between them. Seen from above this control appears rectangular but if the struts and supporting bars are jointed flexibily the animals may be turned to face sideways as well as forwards. The ball throwing movement is described later in a section on juggling puppets.

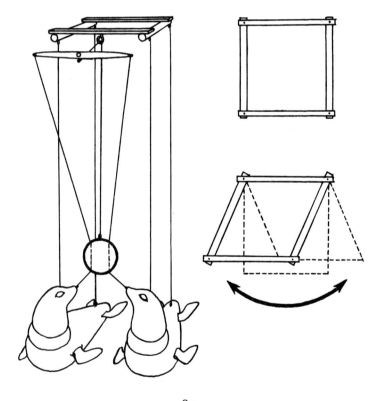

Seven circus marionettes

The seven circus marionettes described in the following pages are chosen partly because they are particular favourites of mine, and also because they display between them most of the mechanisms found in trick puppetry. Here are seen practical applications of vertical, horizontal, tip-up, and irregular controls; puppets with freely moving joints, and puppets moving in a restricted plane.

Some of these puppets, with little or no change of mechanism, can be presented quite differently. The weight lifter turns easily into a pole balancer, while the tricks of the juggler clown can be used by individual animals standing on their hind legs, or by animals in pairs on a tandem control. The mechanism of the circus horse can be adapted or simplified for almost any animal in the puppet circus, and the dancer on the tight rope may well be transferred to horseback, with her toe attached to the saddle. The principle of threading hand and foot strings through apparatus, used for the trapeze acrobat and the weight lifter, is the basis of many further tricks.

From these beginnings it should be possible to develop dozens of different types of circus puppet. Experiment can be made by planning on paper, but more successfully through trial and error stringing of small jointed figures.

Figure 47   Ringmaster

82

The ring master is the only marionette in the puppet circus who may be described as a 'standard' puppet. The way in which any puppet is made and strung depends on the part he has to play, and the ring master has only to walk, bow, and gesture with hands and head. Most acrobatic puppets do all these things in addition to their own trick movements, so a description of the mechanism and stringing of the ring master will serve as a basis for all. For reasons of space I have drawn diagrams of stringing and movements throughout with shorter stringing than would be used for a marionette operated from the leaning bar.

Since the ring master is fully clothed there is no need for elaborate carving of legs and arms; sections of wooden dowel beneath substantial clothing will serve perfectly well. Simple string jointing at shoulder and elbow allows flexible movement, while the wrist joint should be made with the extra sideways movement of the screw eye and wire shaft joint described in the section on irregular jointing. One hand is carved or modelled in a closed position to hold the whip. Waist, thighs, knees, and ankles can all be leather jointed. This is the easiest joint to make, and it works without making any sound.

I have designed the ring master with a bulky figure in contrast to the other circus performers. This does not mean that the chest and pelvis parts must necessarily be made extra large; this would add too much to the puppet's weight. The bulk is added by two loosely hung cushions of padding fixed to the chest piece in front and behind, and the clothes are cut from material which has sufficient substance of its own not to hang too revealingly on the dowel limbs.

The ring master's hat and whip are both additions to the 'standard' marionette. Hats for string puppets are often a problem as they can interfere with stringing. Sometimes they are carved or modelled as part of the head, but to avoid extra weight it is often better to make them separately in cardboard covered with material. This sort of hat should be glued firmly to the head with the head strings passing through the brim.

The ring master's whip is in two parts, the lower being made of stout wire or thin wooden rod which is firmly fixed to one of the puppet's hands. This hand should be strung higher than the other with the whip handle, weighted at the end, just touching the floor. The flexible end of the whip is most successfully made from leather thonging stiffened into a curve at the handle end with shellac or glue. The joint is concealed by whipped carpet thread.

Articulated mouth   Figure 48

The ring master is the only speaking member of the puppet circus as it is his job to introduce the different acts of his performers. An articulated mouth is not necessary in all speaking marionettes—it often leads to the placing of a false emphasis on the face rather than on the whole body. However with the ring master additional mouth movement adds contrast to the other purely acrobatic puppets.

When an articulated mouth is used, it must be part of the design of the head from the very beginning. The mechanism is more suited to the folds and lines of a middle aged face than a young one, and the head should be made hollow with plenty of room for inside mechanism.

84

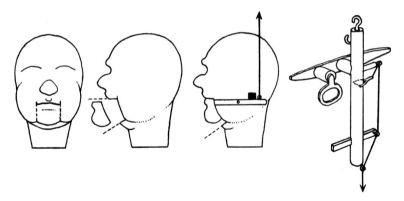

Figure 48   Articulated mouth

The diagram above shows how two vertical cuts are made in the completed head from the corners of the mouth downwards as far as the neck. Two further cuts, across the front of the neck and between the upper and lower lip, free the lower mouth and chin piece which is removed and trimmed smooth. The back of the head is also removed so that work can be carried out inside.

A wooden tongue on a wire shaft is fitted into the head. The tongue lies horizontally from front to back of the head, level with the back of the lower lip to which it is fixed with plastic wood. The ends of the shaft are greased, and bedded in plastic wood on each inner side of the head; they move freely when the plastic wood is dry. The rear half of the wooden tongue is weighted, keeping the puppet's mouth in a closed position, and a string from the back of the tongue passes through the top of the puppet's head, up the control bar to a wire lever on the main shaft. Downwards pressure on the lever from the third finger of the operator's supporting hand opens and closes the puppet's mouth. The range of mouth movement depends on the amount of space removed between the back of the chin and the neck.

Strings used for marionettes may vary in thickness from macramé twine to fine carpet thread depending on the size and weight of the puppet. The length of the strings is decided by the height of the marionette, the type of control bar used, and the distance between the leaning rail and stage floor of your theatre. The height of the manipulator also must be taken into consideration. For string puppets 450 mm high I usually find that shoulder strings 1200 mm long are sufficient.

In wooden marionettes strings are attached to small screw-eyes fixed in appropriate positions on the control bar and in the puppet itself. In papier mâché puppets wire loops are included in the framework, while the strings of cloth puppets can be sewn in position on the actual cloth.

Before starting to attach the strings the control bar is hung at the height decided on for the length of stringing. The shoulder strings are attached first, and all other strings measured and tied in relation to them. The hands are usually strung slightly raised, and the knees really taut so that any movement of the leg bar has instant response.

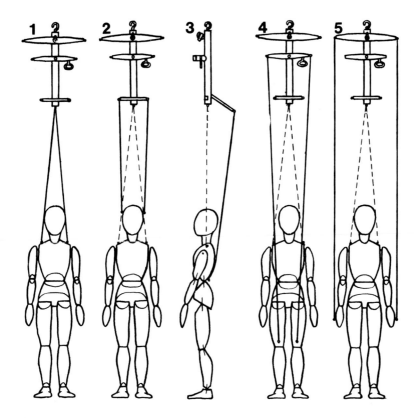

Figure 49

1   *Shoulder strings* These must be equal in length so that the puppet hangs in an evenly balanced position.
2   *Head strings* The screw eyes in the head are placed slightly behind and above the ear. This is important for head turning movements.
3   *Back string* The screw eye in the back is placed just above the waist joint. This string with the shoulder strings keeps the puppet under steady control.
4   *Knee strings* The screw eyes for these strings are placed just above the knee joint. Knee strings must be tied taut.
5   *Hand strings* These are usually tied on the thumb side of the hand, so that the hand is raised in a sideways position.

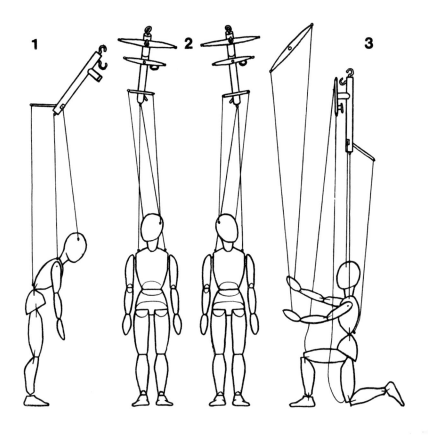

Simple movements   Figure 50

1   *Bowing* The control bar is tilted forward while the point of the bowing string attachment stays level. The shoulder and head strings lower the puppet forward from the waist.

2   *Head turning* This results from a slight forwards and sideways tilt of the control bar. The forward tilt allows the head to fall forward. The side-ways tilt slackens one head string and tightens the other, pulling the head to one side.

3   *Kneeling on one knee* A downwards movement of the thumb in the leg bar raises and bends the puppet's right knee while the whole crutch is moved forward and lowered. The hands follow the angle of the raised hand bar.

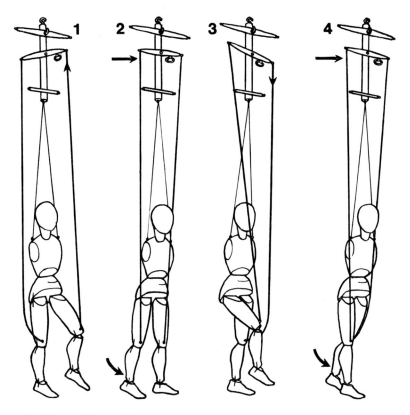

Walking   Figure 51

1   The upward movement of the thumb in the leg bar
slackens the right string and raises the left knee.

2   The whole control bar moves forward over the left leg
which straightens as the leg bar returns to position. The right
leg closes beside the left partly from gravity, and partly from
the beginning of the next movement.

3   The downwards movement of the thumb raises the right
knee.

4   The control bar moves forward over the right leg while
the left swings to close beside the other. Although walking
is described here in stages, the forward movement of the
control bar is smooth and continuous.

Figure 52   Juggler

These are among the easier of circus puppets to make and manipulate, and three varieties are described here. In the first only one ball is used, but although this may not strictly be called juggling, the trick is most effective. As the ball is thrown into the air and caught by each hand in turn, it rises higher and higher and may finally disappear. In a comedy act, the ball can stay out of sight for as long as the operator wishes, and then return unexpectedly. A second juggler uses two balls which are thrown up alternately giving an illusion of juggling although the balls do not actually change hands. In a third trick two balls are again used, but in addition to the movements of the previous trick, they may be bounced on to the puppet's forehead and left foot.

These three tricks are described in stages, but in performance the movements are continuous and flowing. Practice in front of a mirror shows the manipulator what is actually happening; this is not easily seen from above.

Juggling puppets should be made with heads slightly tilted back, and eyes raised as if to follow the movement of the balls. The type of jointing used in body and legs is open to choice, but the arms should be as flexible as possible. I find that a string joint at shoulder and elbow works well here, while leather hinge joints at the wrists stand up best to the wear and tear of jerking hand strings. The balls can be made from table tennis balls, split and weighted inside with plastic wood, and the palms of the juggler's hands should be lined with felt to deaden sound.

The main control bar of the juggler is of standard type, so the puppet may walk, bow, or jump about in addition to doing his tricks. The juggling movements are controlled by a detachable hand bar (or bars) whose strings pass down through the balls to the puppet's hands, forehead or toes.

Puppet jugglers soon exhaust the number of tricks which they can do, and are most entertaining to an audience when presented in groups, making full use of contrast, competition, and sound effects.

1   The hand bar is shown in position on the main control, with the ball resting in the juggler's hands. Strings from each end of the bar run through the ball to the palms, while a third string from the centre of the bar is attached to the ball itself.

2   When the juggler is walking the hand bar should be detached and held forward to allow free movement of the knee strings.

3   The centre string of the hand bar is looped over its hook and the bar sharply tilted to the right, throwing the ball from one hand into the air.

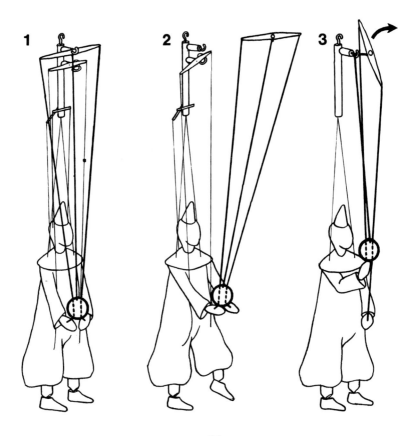

Figure 53b

4 As the hand bar is levelled and moved forward, the centre string draws the ball into the air. The further forward the bar is moved, the higher the ball rises.

5 The hand bar returns close to the main control and is tilted to the left, raising the left hand to catch the ball as it runs down the taut string.

6 The left hand is lowered, and the ball falls back to its first position. The sequence can now be repeated in reverse starting with the left hand, or the ball may be thrown into the air by both hands together.

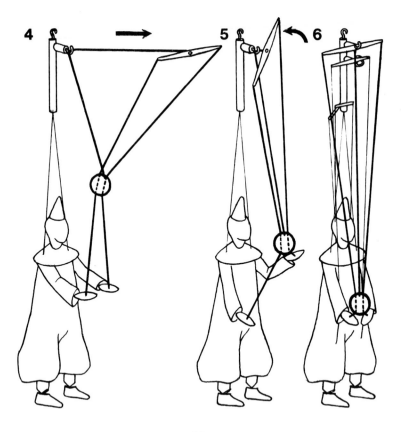

G

Figure 54

1 In this second trick two balls are used. Strings from the ends of the hand bar are threaded through each ball to the palms of the hands.

2 When the hand bar is jerked sharply from side to side, each ball is thrown into the air in turn, and falls back down its string into place.

3 If the hand bar is turned end-on towards the audience, the balls appear to be thrown from hand to hand.

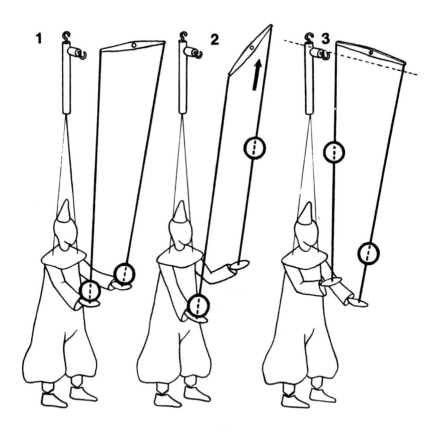

Figure 55
1 A third juggling trick uses an extra bar with strings
through each ball to the puppet's forehead and left foot.
Since the two bars are held in separate hands, the puppet,
after making his entrance, must be supported by a second
manipulator or hung from a bracket over the stage.
2 A sharp jerk on the hand bar sends both balls into the air.
3 The hand bar is lowered, the second bar raised, and the
balls run back down the taut strings onto the juggler's forehead and left foot. The ball on the foot returns to the left
hand by reversing the same movements, while the forehead
ball returns by its own weight.

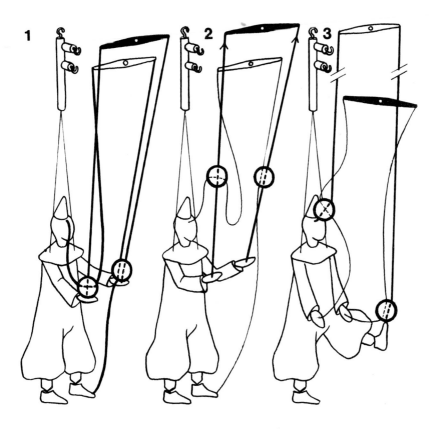

Figure 56   Trapeze acrobat

The acrobat described here makes his entrance hanging by his hands on a spinning trapeze which is lowered from above. As it reaches the ground he bows to the audience, and rises into the air again as the trapeze begins to swing, raising and lowering his legs to increase the arc of movement. After several swings he raises his feet to the bar, releases his hands, and hangs by the feet alone. Still swinging he returns to the hand hold position and raises himself waist high to the bar, alternately raising and lowering himself by the arms. Finally, from the toe hold position, he rises to stand on the still moving bar.

This puppet is simply constructed and moves in a vertical plane only. From shoulder to finger-tip the arms are made in one piece, the palms of the hands being curved to fit round the bar. The shoulders pivot on a wire shaft through the chest, and the head, neck and upper body are made in one. The waist is a leather joint which bends forward only, as backward movement is limited by a canvas strip joining the chest and stomach. The thigh joints should allow no sideways movement, and although the knees may be jointed, the legs can be made in one piece from the thigh joint to the toes which are pointed downwards.

The trapeze is made from an upper and lower wooden dowel bar joined on each side by lengths of rigid wire. The wire ends are turned in and fixed to the lower bar allowing no rotation, but are looped and free swinging from grooves in the upper bar.

The main control bar is irregular, being T-shaped and exactly half the height of the acrobat himself from toes to finger tips when he stands with arms raised. The lower end of the T-bar is fixed to the centre of the upper trapeze bar, and when not in use the control is hung in position number 4 of the following diagrams. From each side of the cross stroke of the T-bar strings of equal length pass down through holes in the lower trapeze bar to screw-eyes in the palms of the acrobat's hands, and on his toes. The toe strings pass in

97

front of the upper trapeze bar, the hand strings behind.

A fifth string runs from the top centre of the T-bar down behind the trapeze to the top of the acrobat's head. For most of the time this string hangs loose, but should be measured to be of equal tension with the hand strings when the acrobat is in position 5.

Figure 57a

1 With the T-bar control bent forward to its limit, the acrobat makes his entrance in this position hanging from the trapeze by his hands. The trapeze is spun round on a string loop, and lowered from above to the centre of the stage as if descending from the top of the circus tent.

2 As the puppet's feet touch the ground, the trapeze stops spinning and the string loop is discarded. The trapeze is lowered still further and the acrobat makes his bow facing the audience. The extended toes push the body backwards at the thigh joint, and the head bends forward between the shoulders.

3 The trapeze is lifted into the air and turned sideways. Alternate raising and lowering of the T-bar to mid position raises and lowers the acrobat's legs, giving momentum to the trapeze as it begins to swing from side to side. From now on the operator continues to support and swing the trapeze with one hand, and move the T-bar control with the other.

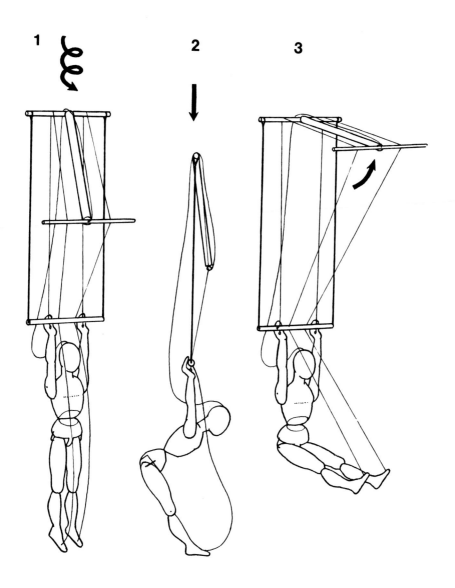

Figure 57b

4 With the trapeze still swinging, the T-bar is raised upright, bringing the acrobat's feet up to the level of his hands.

5 As the T-bar is bent backward to mid-position, the acrobat's hands drop away from the trapeze, and he is left hanging by the toes alone. This is the only position of the T-bar control in which the head string is stretched taut.

4

5

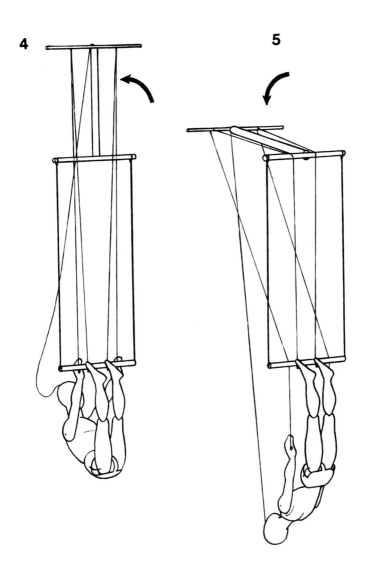

Figure 57c
6   With the T-bar bent fully backwards, the acrobat's hands stretch down beyond his head. While the trapeze continues to swing, all these movements may be reversed to bring the acrobat back to his original position, hanging from the trapeze by his hands.
7   Here, starting from position 3, the head string is raised until the acrobat balances his weight on the trapeze with his arms. His hands slide round to the top of the trapeze bar pushing the handstrings to one side. While the operator raises the head string his other hand must support and swing the trapeze, keeping the T-bar in position at the same time. The head string may also be used when the acrobat is in position 5 raising him to standing position on the trapeze bar with his hands by his sides! This is not easy to do, as the foot strings must be loosened slightly (by raising the T-bar to a vertical and slightly forward position) before the feet will slide round to the top of the trapeze bar.

6

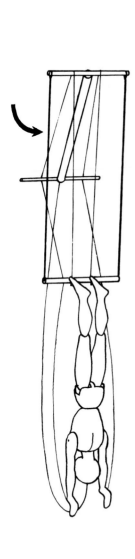

7

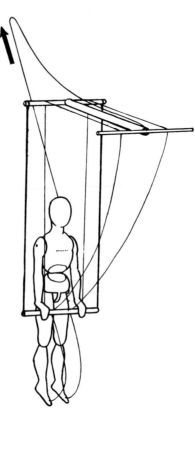

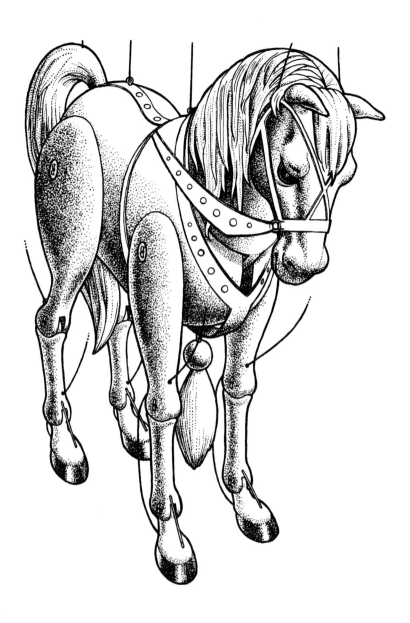

Figure 58   Trotting horse

In a puppet circus the horse is by far the most effective of animal performers. Lions, tigers and elephants whose tricks are in fact very limited, hold the attention of a real circus audience by the degree of danger to which their trainers are exposed, and this element is lost in the puppet theatre. The horse, however, performs beyond the knowledge of many spectators, and its puppet counterpart carries out many of the classical school movements of *haute école*.

The horse described here can trot, canter, leap over jumps, rear on its hind legs, paw the ground with its hooves, raise and lower its head and tail, and kick with its back legs. Its movements are best shown in a circular track round the centre rostrum described in a later chapter on theatres. However, its individual head, foot and tail control (to which the ears may easily be added) make it a good partner to the ringmaster in the favourite old circus act of the 'talking horse' which answers questions and counts with movements of head and forefeet.

In making the horse, a careful plan should work out front and side profiles of the various parts with the position of the joints *(see figure 59)*. The body, cut from balsa wood to reduce weight, is simple in shape and easily pared and sandpapered. Balsa wood, however, will not hold screw eyes, so the strings supporting the main weight of the horse are attached to loops at each end of a single wire which passes right through the body, along the belly underneath and up again. The legs, having no weight to bear, may be cut as slender as you like, the upper legs from flat sections of soft-wood and the lower legs from wooden dowelling. Where they join the body the legs pivot on fixed wire shafts running from side to side. All other joints, including the neck, are tongue and groove joints with no sideways movement. Knee action should be limited to one direction only, backwards at the front knees, and forwards at each knee (stifle) of the rear legs.

The trotting horse has a standard horizontal animal control bar, with two projecting leg bars on either side. Because of the narrowness of the shoulder only one string runs to each front leg, passing through it just above the knee joint, and running down behind to join the back of the hoof. This stringing tucks each hoof well under the raised knee in the characteristic trotting movement. Each rear leg bar has one direct and one cross string. The direct string runs to the back of the knee, the cross string to the opposite leg passing through it just above the ankle (hock) and ending in the back of the hoof. The tail is strung through the end of the main control bar and fixed to a movable wooden button. The head is held erect by two strings from behind the ears which join together below the control and finish in a short length of strong elastic or wire spring. Finally, short lengths of round elastic or tiny springs are attached across the front of each hock from just above the joint to the centre of the hoof. This prevents the hooves from dropping to a 'tiptoe' position.

Figure 59

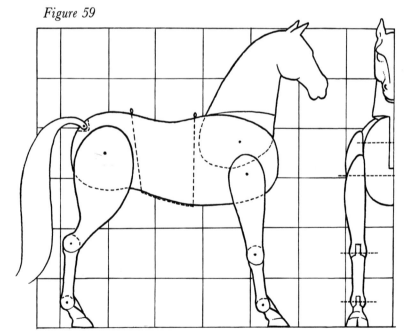

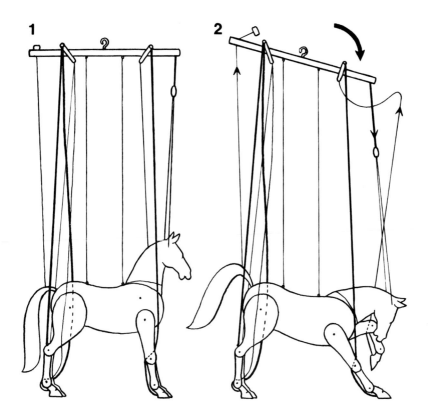

Figure 60a

1   In the standing position the main control bar is held level. All strings are of equal tension except for the cross strings to the hind legs which are loose. For the 'Spanish Trot' (straight forward foreleg raising) the foreleg stringing is altered to pass through the leg just above the hock.

2   When the main control is tilted down at the front, the horse's body alters position to the same angle. Individual movements show the raising of the tail button to lift the tail, the raising of a foreleg string to bend front knee and ankle, and the stretching of the elastic section of the head string to lower the head.

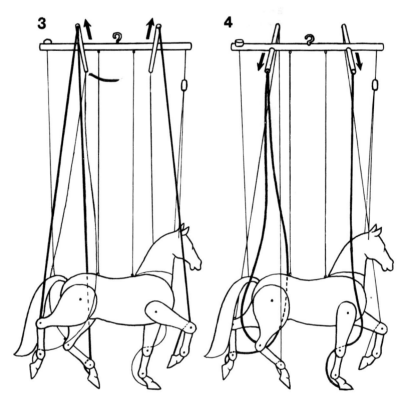

Figure 60b

3   This is stage one of the trotting movement which is
carried out by alternate side to side rotation of the main bar.
The strings from the raised near side leg bars lift the rear
leg backwards and the front leg forwards. The cross string
to the far back leg raises it forward.

4   The main control bar is now rotated in the opposite
direction, moving the horse into the second position of the
trot and continues forward, rising slightly up and down
between each change. In the 'passage' (slow trot with bent
knees) the rotation dwells for a moment at its limit on each
side. This may be done to music.

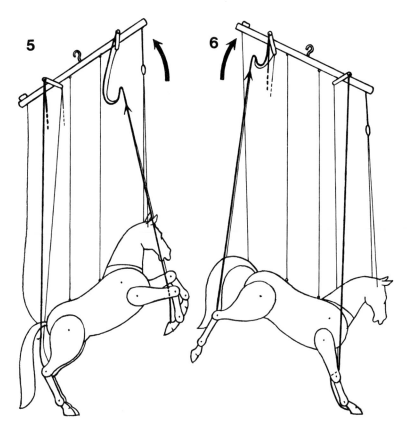

Figure 60c

5　As the foreleg strings are gathered together and raised, an upward tilt of the front of the main control moves the horse into a rearing position or 'levade'. A series of forward jumps on the hind legs alone is known as the 'courbette'. This same position guides the horse to leap over an obstacle following a canter which is carried out by rocking the main control forward and backwards with no sideways movement.

6　For a backward kick the main control bar is raised at the back, and the direct rear leg strings are gathered together and jerked sharply.

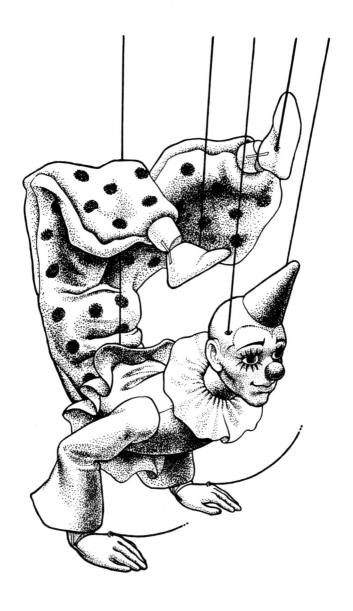

Figure 61 *Hand-balancing acrobat*

The hand-balancer makes his entrance in a series of jumps, standing upright on his feet. He bows to the audience, bends over from the waist to place his hands on the floor, and balancing on his palms, slowly raises his legs until his feet are straight up above his head. In this position he raises and lowers himself a few times by bending and straightening his elbows, and raises and lowers his feet, or kicks them alternately above his head. Finally, moving one hand at a time he walks round the stage on his hands. This puppet is designed to move in one plane only with no sideways movement except at the neck. Both hands and feet must be weighted, and if the puppet is clothed in clown's costume, wooden dowel limbs may be used with leather hinge joints throughout. The waist, thigh and ankle joints move freely backwards and forwards, but knee, wrist and elbow bend in one direction only. The shoulder joint rotates on a wire shaft passing through the chest from side to side.

Figure 62
The main control bar is a tip-up control. A detachable foot
bar with strings to the insteps is placed behind the base of the
main bar, and a wire lever with strings to the back of the
acrobat's hands is placed in the front centre. Head strings
from a fixed bar at the top of the main control support most
of the puppet's weight along with a string from the base of
the main bar which runs to the acrobat's back. When the
main control is tipped forward the index finger of the
supporting hand raises the hand string lever forward
between the head strings. *(A)* This stringing is irregular but
quite simple, and avoids the complication of knee strings for
upright walking movement.

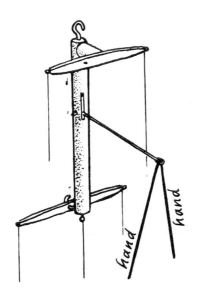

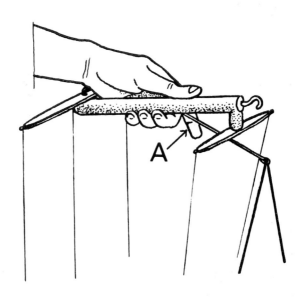

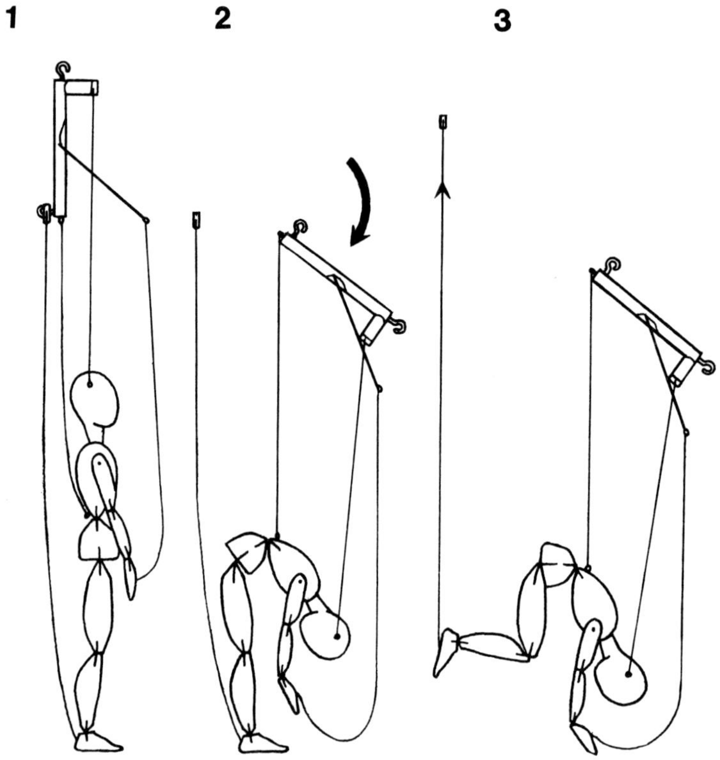

Figure 63a

1   In the normal standing position most of the weight is taken by the head strings. The hand string lever lies in resting position with its strings hanging loose.

2   With the leg bar detached, the main control is tipped over to allow the top half of the puppet to bend down. The hand string lever is moved forward between the head strings by the index finger of the supporting hand.

3   The weighted hands of the acrobat touch the ground and the leg bar is raised, bringing the feet up. The acrobat settles on to the palms of his hands.

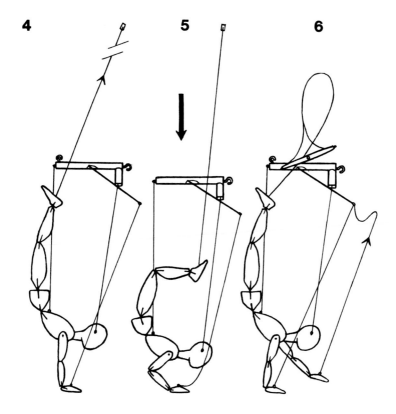

Figure 63b

4 As the leg bar rises further, its strings pass on either side of the main control bar, and the legs on either side of the back string. The main control is levelled, lifting the head and reversing the arch of the back.

5 Movement of the main control makes the acrobat appear to push himself up and down on his hands. The leg bar may be used to raise or lower the legs or to make them kick in turn.

6 The foot bar and its strings, keeping the legs extended, are gathered into the supporting hand, while the free hand moves the hand strings alternately as the acrobat walks forward on his palms.

Figure 64　Tight rope dancer

I have combined in this circus puppet the movements of a
ballet dancer and a tight rope walker. The progression of the
traditional tight rope walking marionette along his rope is
never very convincing as neither foot can pass the other and
the result is only a sideways shuffle. The series of hops and
turns on one toe by which the dancer moves appear to me
much more natural.

The tight rope dancer makes her entrance on a rigid wire
previously stretched between two fixed points out of sight
of the audience on either side of the stage. With arms
undulating before her, and one leg raised sideways she crosses
to the centre of the rope in a series of hops on one pointed toe
and moves into an arabesque position, bending forward
from the hips with one leg raised high behind her. Returning
to her entrance position the dancer hops to the far side of the
tight rope, lowers her arms and leg and spins round on one
toe in a pirouette; as she spins faster and faster, her arms and
free leg rise sideways, and her skirt flares round about her.
Crossing and recrossing the tight rope the dancer hops on
one toe, pirouettes, and poses in arabesque, until finally
returning to the centre of the stage she sinks down with one
leg stretched along the rope and the other hanging below,
leaning forward from the waist to lay her arms and head
towards the outstretched foot. Combinations of these movements carried out to music can make an effective and artistic
performance.

The dancer is made with each leg in one piece from thigh
to extended toe. The thigh joint of the leg which is attached
to the wire is a leather hinge with forward movement only,
while the other leg is rounded at the thigh and moves quite
freely on a short wire loop between two screw eyes. The
pelvis section on this side is cut away at an angle to allow the
leg to move freely upwards, downwards, forwards, backwards and to the one side. The waist joint is hinged to move
both forwards and backwards, while the shoulder joint is a
loose string joint. The elbow and wrist, being visible, are

tongue and groove jointed, the wrist moving both forwards and backwards with the palms of the hands downwards. The toe on one of the dancer's legs is attached to the tight rope by a thin wire loop long enough to allow the hopping movement, and curved backwards so that the leg may be extended along the tight rope. The wire loop is fixed to the toe in a way which allows the dancer to rotate on the rope while the loop stays in position (see figure 65).

That part of the main control bar which supports the weight of the dancer is of standard design, but the detachable hand bar has side struts providing strings to the mid forearms as well as to the back of each hand. This bar allows a very fluid movement where wrists may be lowered at the end of raised arms. The single leg bar string to the dancer's free foot is quite irregular, being a loosely hung swinging rod closely related in length and movement to the leg which it controls. This bar is held in position between the fingers of the manipulator's supporting hand, leaving the other hand free to hold the hand bar.

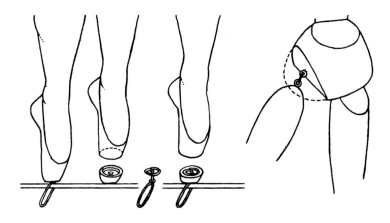

Figure 65   Dancer's toe and hip joint

Figure 66a

1   Before the dancer makes her entrance the end of the tight
rope wire is passed through the loop at the bottom of the
dancer's foot and fixed in place. The hand bar is detached
and tilted so that the hands are raised and the wrists dropped.
When the hand bar is rocked the arms undulate from the
elbow.

2   In the pirouette the hand bar is replaced and the foot
bar hangs free. The whole main control bar is spun round
by its hanging hook, and the dancer's arms and leg swing
outwards with the movement.

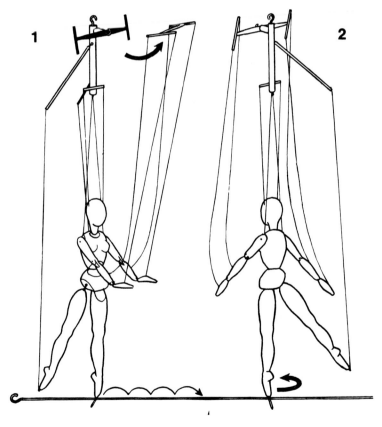

Figure 66b

3   In the arabesque position the main control bar tilts the dancer forward from the waist and the leg bar raises the free leg high behind. The hand bar moves forward to stretch out the arms, and is tilted so that the wrists are raised and the hands hang downwards. In this position a careful manipulator may turn the dancer slowly round on one toe, always remembering that the dancer in arabesque position looks best from the side view. Also, starting from this position, the dancer may be raised erect, and the free leg swung round sideways until it stretches forward in front under raised arms.

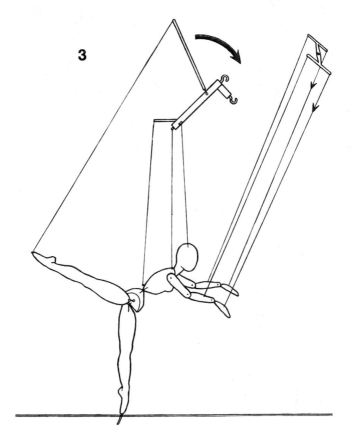

4 The main control bar is lowered so that the dancer's attached leg lies along the wire and the free leg hangs downward. If the dancer is placed so that the wire passes between the division of the legs, she should stay firmly in place. The hand bar moves forward to stretch out the arms towards the dancer's foot.

5 The main control bar is tilted forward and lowered further until the tight rope wire is supporting most of the dancer's weight.

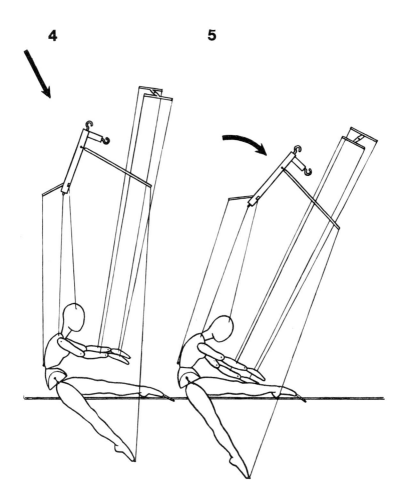

4   **5**

Figure 67   Weight lifter

This is one of the most intricate and entertaining of the circus puppets. The weight-lifter can walk onto the stage, lay his dumb-bells on the floor, and if the hand strings are long enough, rise from a kneeling position and bow to the audience. He can then lift up his weights and, with the appearance of tremendous effort, alternately raise and lower them from a kneeling or standing position. Further stringing makes it possible for this puppet to lie on his back, pass the dumb-bells from his hands to his feet, and raise and lower them with his legs.

The exposed limbs of the weight-lifter demand more careful carving or modelling than is necessary for a puppet in clown's costume. Circus tights of white stockingette cover the joints, but for appearance sake knees and elbows should be made with the concealed hinge described in an earlier chapter. To prevent unnecessary movement all other joints should be firm tongue and groove hinge joints, with a close leather hinge at the waist. The thigh joints, also leather, should be made slightly loose so that the feet move a little apart in raising the dumb-bells. The shoulder joint can be either a close knotted string joint, or it may pivot on a wire shaft passing through the body from side to side.

The main control bar is of standard type with a detachable hand bar and extra foot bar to carry out the weight lifting movements. The wooden dowel shaft of the dumb-bells is pierced vertically for hand and foot strings which pass through it to screw-eyes in the palms of the hands and at the toes. The weights should be heavy enough to remain still on the floor when the hand strings are moving through them.

The presentation of this puppet should be based on the slow and deliberate movements of the real life performance, imitating the stance of the body, and the final quick thrust of the arms as the weights reach the above head position. The feeling of effort can be exaggerated by an accompanying drum roll and final clash of cymbals.

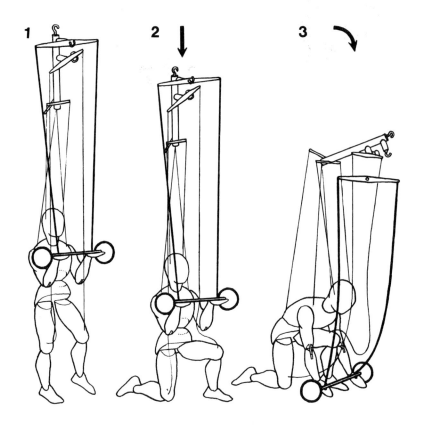

Figure 68a

1   The leg bar is worked by the thumb of the supporting hand as the weight-lifter walks onto the stage to make his bow. With the hand bar in position on the main control, the dumb-bells are held at mid-height.

2   The leg bar is tilted to bring one knee forward, and the whole puppet is advanced and lowered into kneeling position.

3   The main control is tilted so that the puppet leans forward from the waist. The hand bar is detached and lowered so that the hands reach the floor, and the dumb-bells rest on the stage.

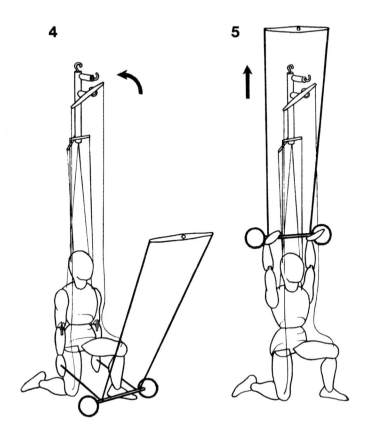

Figure 68b

4 With the hand bar still lowered, the main control is straightened, and the puppet's arms fall back to his sides. The dumb-bells remain in position as the hand strings run through the holes in the shaft.

At this stage the last two movements are repeated as the weight-lifter leans forward to pick up the dumb-bells which return to his hands as the hand bar draws the strings taut once more.

5 The weight-lifter has now returned to kneeling position, and as he kneels or stands the hand bar alternately raises and lowers his weights.

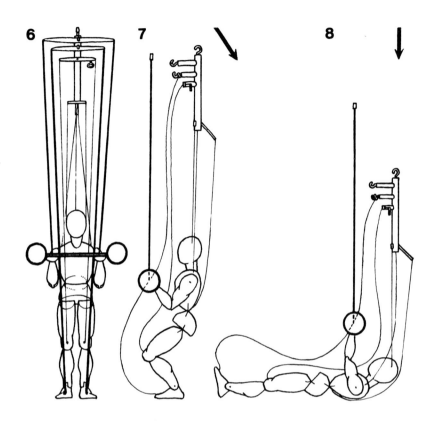

Figure 68c

6   The addition of a foot bar with strings running to the toes through the shaft of the dumb-bells between the handstrings increases the variety of movements which the weight-lifter can do. If the puppet is to be able to perform from a kneeling position, the foot-strings should hang slightly loose when the weight-lifter is standing.

7   The hand bar is detached and held forwards, while the main control bar is lowered and moved backwards.

8   The puppet is now lying on his back, with head slightly raised. The hand bar is used to alternately raise and lower the dumb-bells.

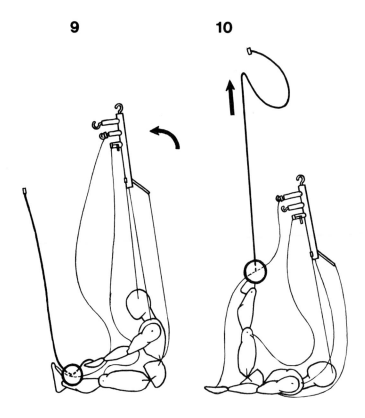

9   **10**

Figure 68d
9 The main control bar now raises the weight-lifter from
the waist. The hand bar moves the arms forward, and a
slight jerk and loosening of the hand strings tips the dumb-
bells on to the puppet's toes. This exchange must be carefully
done so that no loose strings fall round the ends of the weights.
10 The loosened hand bar is replaced on the main control
and the foot bar is detached and raised so that its taut
strings hold the dumb-bells in position on the feet. As the
weight-lifter lies back, the leg bar alternately raises and
lowers the dumb-bells.

Presenting a performance

PUPPET THEATRES

The purpose of a puppet theatre is to concentrate attention on a defined acting area, and to screen from the audience those mechanisms of staging (including manipulators) which the producer wishes to conceal. Both these aims are concerned with creating illusion but are not always necessary. The manipulators of the puppets of the Japanese Bunraku theatre are entirely visible as they move the limbs of their jointed puppets by hand, and the dramatic effect of their production is not lessened. However, in the case of circus puppets where much of the interest lies in trying to guess how the tricks are done, I feel that there must be some concealment.

A puppet theatre can be improvised from folding screens, chairs and curtain material, or it may be a portable or permanent theatre involving carpentry work. The design of your theatre will depend on the type of puppets used. Generally speaking these may be divided into two groups; puppets worked from below (glove, rod and shadow) and puppets worked from above (marionettes).

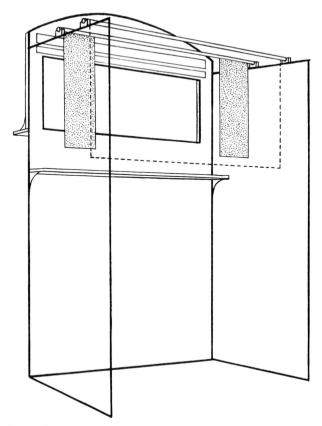

A theatre for puppets worked from below   *Figure 69*

Any theatre for puppets worked from below follows the principles shown in the above drawing. The front screen may be as wide as you like depending on the number of manipulators taking part at one time, but the height is most conveniently designed where the lower border is 1650 mm above the ground at the operator's eye level. The height of the stage opening itself depends on the size of the puppets in use. Glove puppets vary little in size and for them 550 mm may be sufficient. Other types of puppet may well need more height. When shadow puppets are used, the shadow screen is fitted into the stage opening and a light placed behind.

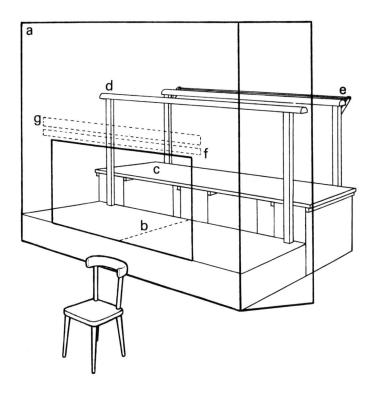

A theatre for puppets worked from above   *Figure 70*

A theatre for puppets worked from above is more complicated. My drawing shows features common to improvised, portable, or permanent theatres of this type.

A   *A screen* or *proscenium* must be high enough to conceal manipulators, with a stage opening at a level visible to a seated audience. In your actual structure this may be only 450 mm above the floor, but the whole theatre may be raised on a rostrum, usually available in church, school or public halls.

B   *A stage floor* is level with the lower border of the stage opening. This floor may be as wide as you like from side to side, but the depth from back to front is seldom more than 900 mm as the operators' arms can reach no further.

C   A bridge is placed behind the stage floor, giving height to the manipulators who stand over their work. The level of the bridge floor is usually 450 mm above the stage but this may vary. The bridge forms the rear limit of the stage, and back-cloths can be hung against it.

D   A leaning bar is fixed to the stage side of the bridge. This protects the operators from falling onto the stage, and can be used as an arm rest.

E   A perch bar is fixed to the back of the bridge, and marion-ettes are hung from it when not in use.

F   A curtain rail on a batten is placed above the stage side of the proscenium opening.

G   A row of light bulbs on a batten is placed above the curtain batten.

Figure 71 (overleaf)
There is no need to be confined by the conventional floor pattern described above. A different disposition of stage floor and divided bridge can deepen the acting area. (See *A*, *B and C*). The layout of *C* is particularly suitable for circus performances as puppet animals can move in a circle round the manipulator as if in a real circus ring. In some permanent theatres the bridge may be built not behind but over the acting area, allowing puppets to be worked from either side. Sometimes an extra bridge may be placed over the front of the stage immediately behind the proscenium screen so that puppets can be handed backwards and forwards between two bridges.

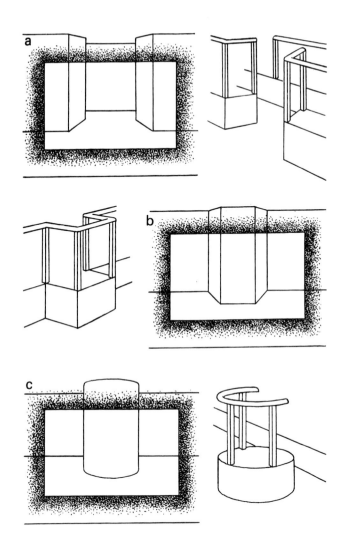

Figure 71

The layout of scenery in the puppet theatre must be very simple as all possible space is needed for the performers. Two basic settings are used behind the proscenium opening in the live theatre; these are the wing setting and the box setting, and each has some application in puppetry.

The wing setting is most suitably used in the theatre for puppets worked from below. Wings are cut in profiles or left plain, and hung from wooden rods resting on the side walls of the theatre frame, while the back cloth hangs from the rod nearest to the back of the theatre. Puppets are placed behind the wings from below, and appear as if entering from the side. An example of this setting is shown in the illustration of the theatre for puppets worked from below.

In a string puppet theatre a wing setting interferes with the strings, and it is safer to depend on a wide backcloth extending beyond the limits of the proscenium opening. Backcloths are kept rolled on wooden rods, and hung when in use on hooks fixed to the supports of the leaning rail.

The box setting encloses the acting area all round like the walls of a room, with doors cut out for entrance and exit. This setting is quite suitable for the theatre for puppets worked from below but can only be used with marionettes when entrance doorways are cut right to the top to allow the passage of strings. In either setting the stage floor of the marionette theatre should be covered with a cloth to hide carpentry joints and to deaden sound.

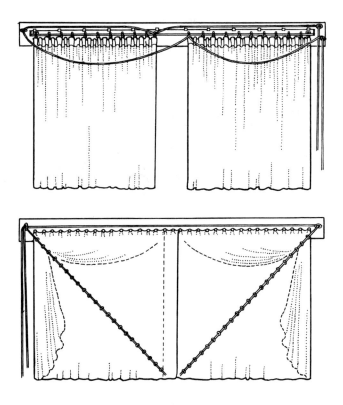

Figure 72 ABOVE *Draw curtains and* BELOW *drape curtains*

Scenery and properties for puppet productions must naturally be in scale with the puppets performing. Properties can be made of the same materials as the puppets themselves —cardboard, papier mâché, and wood. Scenery can be made of thick cardboard with wood framing where necessary, and backcloths from old sheets. Large amounts of paint may have to be used in painting scenery, and I have found that powder paint is cheapest. Mixed with water and a little melted glue size, powder paint stays fixed on cloth and does not rub off. Before painting a sheet backcloth, a coat of diluted size prepares the surface for painting.

Lighting equipment may be ordered through stage lighting suppliers catalogues, or made with help and advice from a local electrician. The important point is to know what you aim to achieve by your lighting, and to carry it out in the most simple, safe and direct method. Always remember that the first object of lighting is to enable the performance to be seen; secondly that by changes of strength and colour the mood and interest of a production can be heightened. The following list of equipment should be sufficient for those who wish to make varied lighting a feature of their production.

1   A hanging batten of light bulbs in reflectors
In puppet theatres of all types this batten is usually placed above the curtain rail behind the proscenium opening. Sometimes the reflectors are fitted with grooves to hold coloured gelatine slides which can be changed between scenes.

2   Individual lamps hanging or placed on stands
These lamps can be floodlamps, or spot lamps to give a concentrated beam. Lamps at the side of the stage help to eliminate shadow, and lamps hanging from brackets in front of the theatre are effective in lighting puppets at the front of the stage where the batten above is less effective.

3   Switchboard and dimmers
A 'suitcase' switchboard with dimmers is made by some stage lighting companies, and is very useful for travelling productions. The switchboard has a separate control for each piece of lighting equipment, and a separate dimmer to vary the light power of each circuit. The whole switchboard is fed from a main plug.

PRODUCTION

The presentation of a circus show is different from that of a straight play at the theatre. The circus has no continuous story to tell, and the attention of its audience cannot be held by a developing plot with changes of mood and emotion. The technical skill of circus performers will always arouse interest and admiration, but any trick puppet, however striking at first sight, will soon exhaust its repertoire. It is the job of a good puppet showman to present his circus acts in a way which makes the most of each puppet over a lengthened period, and keeps the audience constantly entertained by a variety of sights and sounds. The following points should be remembered in planning a show.

Contrast Contrast of any kind prevents monotony. In a circus show slow acts can be placed between faster ones, and performances depending on skill placed between the comedy performances of clowns.

Competition The length of a trick puppet's act can be extended when two identical puppets compete in turn against each other. There are opportunities for comedy here, particularly with jugglers, balancers, and weight lifters.

Climax Most acrobatic puppets are able to do several variations of their main performance. These variations are most effective when presented in order of difficulty. The final and most spectacular trick can be accompanied by a long drum roll and a crash of cymbals.

Continuity Careful arrangement of the different acts of the circus should make sure that the stage is never left empty. The ring-master, who introduces each act, can always remain in sight, when other puppets leave at the end of their performance. If complicated apparatus is being prepared between acts, the stage can be invaded by the more easily managed clowns (stilt-walkers for example).

Sound effects A roll of drums helps to heighten the tension before achievement in any acrobatic turn; the clash of cymbals announces success. In knock-about clown acts, horns, bursting balloons, and again cymbals can underline the action. Clappers may be used for trotting horses.

Music As we have seen, various percussion instruments can help in making sound effects. The rhythm of more developed music-making is very useful with certain acts. When trapeze acrobats or jugglers are performing, one repeated movement remains interesting for a longer period if carried out in time to a musical background. Music can increase in speed as the performance becomes faster and the number of movements to each bar may be doubled. Music performed 'live', easily timed to movements on the stage, is more effective than recorded music which is often incorrect in scale to small puppets.

Colour A circus theme gives great opportunity for bright and contrasting colour schemes in the trappings of horses and the costumes of clowns and acrobats. The glitter of gold and silver sequins and tinsel can be added to the strong reds, oranges, yellows, greens and blues of materials. If the stage and puppets are striking to look at, the performance is already half way to success.

Lighting In many amateur puppet theatres, lighting serves only to make the stage visible in a darkened room. With more elaborate equipment, colour changes add contrast to an act, and extend its interest. Dimming serves little purpose in a circus show which is normally ablaze with light. However, on a darkened stage, small electric torch bulbs fitted to acrobats' apparatus (the trapeze bar for instance) can be very effective. These bulbs are connected to batteries in the control bar by wiring which runs parallel to the supporting strings.

Shadow, rod and glove puppets

Shadow, rod and glove puppets are worked from below, and being 'earth bound' have only a limited application to the circus theme. However, each type of puppet has its own nature, and with reference to the types of leverage described in the section on working toys, some aspects of the circus performance can be found suitable to each.

SHADOW PUPPETS

shown in a darkened room against a transluscent screen with a light behind, can exploit the visual qualities of the circus. If a wide screen is used the whole circus procession can be seen, with elephants, caravans, camels, and horses in great numbers. Colour is added when the card figures are perforated and lined with coloured cellophane.

There are two standard types of shadow puppet *(see figure 73)*.
A This figure rests in position on a ledge at the foot of a forward tilted screen. One rod, held in the manipulator's left hand, supports the puppet at the neck, while two further rods to the puppet's hands are held in the manipulator's

Figure 73   Shadow puppets

right. In moments of rest the supporting rod can be bedded in plasticene on a second lower ledge, leaving the manipulator's left hand free. Since the supporting rods are held at an angle and not flat against the screen, an acrobat puppet of this type can appear to fly through the air.

B   A second type of shadow puppet is supported on a fixed rod and works by leverage alone. Many types of leverage may be used for figures singly or in groups. Both types of shadow puppet are made from card jointed with carpet thread, while rods are made from thick wire, and levers from fuse wire.

ROD PUPPETS *Figure 74*

Some rod puppets are flat, some are made solid like marionettes, and some are closely related to glove puppets. Each is supported on a rod from below with two extra rods for the hands. While shadow puppets can be effective at a height of only 200 mm, rod puppets are usually much larger being 500 mm and more in height. They tend to be slow and deliberate in gesture, depending for dramatic effect on individual movements of head, hands, and features, and to plan a circus performance with rod puppets is in many ways to neglect their true nature. However, flat rod puppets can make use of the same methods of leverage as shadow puppets, and have the extra detail and colour of painted features and costumes.

GLOVE PUPPETS *Figure 75*

Glove puppet bodies are made in two ways; with arms placed sideways, and with arms facing forwards. Sometimes legs are added free swinging, or with holes for the operator's second hand. Glove puppets are direct and quick in movement, and have the ability to pick up (and throw) small objects. Being closely linked to the operator without the barrier of strings or rods they are highly expressive of personality, although incapable of any kind of acrobatic movement. A circus performance with glove puppets should concentrate on the knock about and noisy performance of the clowns making full use of speech, properties, and sound effects.

141

K

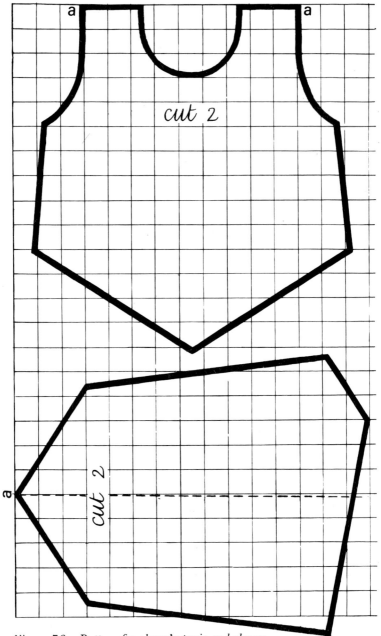

Figure 76   Pattern for clown's tunic and sleeves

Painting and clothing

CLOTHES

In designing clothes for puppets more attention should be given to broad effects of colour, tone and profile, than to detail which cannot be seen at a distance. The choice of material depends on the extent to which the puppet beneath has been carved or modelled; puppets with dowel limbs can be given 'body' by use of materials with substance of their own. Patterned material should be chosen to suit the scale of the puppets themselves.

Clothes become part of the function of the puppet which they cover, concealing the more obvious joints, and giving a fluid appearance to movement. Generally, made by methods of ordinary dress-making, they are added to completed puppets which have been tested for movement. The strings of marionettes have to be untied from the control bar, threaded through the clothes from inside, and then retied from above.

It would be impossible to give patterns for all the clothes which may be met with in a puppet circus, so I have drawn a basic shape for the clown's costume alone, which can be drawn on 15 or 20 mm squared paper for puppets of 45 or

143

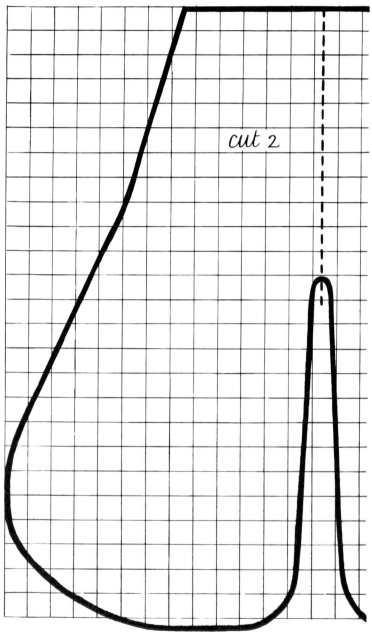

cut 2

Figure 77   Pattern for clown's trousers

60 mm in height. The trousers are attached to the body just below the armpits leaving plenty of room for waist and thigh movement, while the jacket can be completed by a flounce below, and a ruff at the neck. When clothing acrobatic puppets in tights of stretch stockingette, it is best not to sew the shoulder seams at all where the shoulder has been fully modelled, but to turn the cloth inwards gluing it to the inner joint surfaces *(see figures 76 and 77)*.

PAINTING

Before colouring papier mâché or wood, the surface must be prepared to prevent the paint from sinking in. A coat of spirit varnish or clear shellac seals papier mâché or wood, and when dry the surface is glasspapered smooth. Other modelling substances can usually be painted without preparation.

Oil paint and acrylic paint are both waterproof and suitable for most purposes. Oil paint has a translucent quality good for faces and hands; acrylic paint has a harder appearance but is thinned with water and dries quickly.

The colouring of puppets' faces should be bright enough to stand up to stage lighting where it is used, and a strong outline round the eyes helps them to be seen at a distance.

Hair
Hair may be modelled or carved as part of the puppet's head, but when this is done there is no contrast in texture. Real hair, doll's hair, fur or wool are often successfully added to the completed puppet. Sometimes a skull cap is made of stiff material on to which wool or hair can be sewn, and fur or lambs wool can be stretched to the same pattern. When hair is glued directly to the head it is wisest to place it in small overlapping hanks working inwards towards the crown. These same methods of attaching hair may be used for the manes and tails of animals where they have not been included in modelling or carving. Except in the case of glove puppets, the complete covering of animals with fur is seldom successful.

APPENDIX

PLASTIC MODELLING MATERIALS

In the past, papier mâché and occasionally plastic wood have been the accepted plastic modelling materials for puppets. Recently there have appeared on the market new modelling substances suitable for puppetry, which, although more expensive than papier mâché, cut out a lot of preparatory work. I have selected two of these for description, along with the directions for making papier mâché and plastic wood.

PAPIER MÂCHÉ PULP

Papier mâché pulp can be used to line plaster moulds, or for direct modelling of detail over a basis of laminated papier mâché. Newspaper is traditionally used for papier mâché pulp, but I find torn paper towelling cleaner to work with. The amount of pulp needed to line moulds of heads, hands and feet of one puppet can be made from five double sheets of newpaper, or the equivalent amount of any other type of paper.

The paper is torn into very small pieces, about 6 mm square if you have the patience, and left soaking overnight in water. The soaked paper is then thoroughly sifted and rubbed while still in water, removed, squeezed out and kneaded on a slab until it is as smooth in texture as you can make it. This pulp forms the fibrous part of your papier mâché, and to it is added for bulk, modelling clay and ceiling whiting powder, in quarter parts to the volume of paper pulp. Lastly, a teacupful of thick melted glue size is mixed in little by little until the pulp can be rolled in pellets which do not crumble. Flour paste is often used here instead of glue, but the final result is not so strong.

LAMINATED PAPIER MACHE

Laminated papier mâché can be used to line a plaster mould, or directly modelled over a core (from which it may later be cut). Any absorbent paper will do for this type of papier mâché. Sugar paper, paper towelling, or paper handkerchiefs are all suitable, depending on the scale of work to be done. Sugar paper may be bought in different colours, so that layers can be built up evenly, one colour at a time. The paper is soaked before use so that it is malleable, and this is best done in a solution of thin glue size, or diluted office gum. Once soaked and squeezed out, laminated papier mâché is built up in four or five layers, each layer being pasted to the next with thick flour or cold water paste. Paper pieces are torn to fit the shapes required, and paste is used on both sides of each layer. When the layers are complete, the surface is pressed and rubbed smooth with a finger wetted in paste.

If laminated papier mâché is to be removed from a core or mould, the first layer should be placed without paste, and the completed skin removed while still flexible enough to pass over undercuts.

PLASTIC WOOD

Plastic wood is usually bought ready made in tins or tubes, but it can be made from a mixture of glue and fine sawdust by those who have access to a woodwork department. Plastic wood may be used to line moulds (which are previously soaked in water, not greased) or for adding or repairing detail in puppets carved from wood.

MOD-ROC

Mod-roc, produced by Reeves and Sons Limited, Enfield, Middlesex, is a new material for direct modelling made of fine gauze strip impregnated with plaster of paris. Lengths of *Mod-roc* are moistened in water and applied directly over a prepared basic shape. Work may be smoothed and modelled while still moist; final hardening taking place after about 30 minutes. This form of direct modelling can be used in puppetry over a core of wire and bound paper. A thin coat of varnish over completed work should safeguard against chipping, and prepares the surface for painting with oil, acrylic, or poster paints.

BIBLIOGRAPHY

SPECIALISED PUPPETRY
H W Whanslaw and Victor Hotchkiss
Wells Gardner Darton   Redhill Surrey   1948

TRICK MARIONETTES
Nicholas Nelson and J J Hayes
Puppetry Imprints   Birmingham Michigan   1935

ANIMAL MARIONETTES
Paul McPharlin
Puppetry Handbook X
Puppetry Imprints   Birmingham Michigan   1936

PUPPETS INTO ACTORS
Olive Blackham
Rockliff   London   1948

THE MARIONETTE
George Merten
Thomas Nelson   Toronto New York and Edinburgh   1957

SIMPLE TOYMAKING
Sheila Jackson
Studio Vista   London   Watson-Guptill   New York   1966

WOODEN TOY-MAKING
Winifred M Horton
Dryad Press   Leicester   Sixth Edition   1956

CIRCUS
Editors of *Country Beautiful* magazine
Hawthorn Books   New York   1964

SAWDUST AND SPOTLIGHT
Pamela Macgregor-Morris
H F & G Witherby   London   1960

SUPPLIERS

Art and craft shops
Cardboard for properties, scenery, and for making shadow puppets and flat toys. Paper of all thicknesses for plans and tracing. Paste and glue and craft knives. Modelling clay for papier mâché. Plasticine for modelling heads and hands and to aid casting. Powder paint for scenery; poster, acrylic and oil paint for painting puppets and toys of all materials. Cord for string joints; picture framer's pins for leather joints. Sugar paper for laminated papier mâché. Spirit varnish for sealing papier mâché. Paint brushes. Leather for leather joints.

Model kit shops
Wooden dowelling of all thicknesses for marionette control bars and puppets' limbs. Plywood for properties, theatres, animal neck jointing and flat toys. Plastic wood for lining moulds and for fitting special mechanisms inside puppet heads. Wood glues.

Painters' and decorators' shops
Ceiling whiting powder for papier mâché. Glue and size crystals to add to papier mâché or powder paint.

Hardware shops
Wire of all thicknesses for framework for directly-modelled puppets, tongue and groove joints and cotter pins. Broom handles for construction of marionette control bars.

Carpenters' tool shops
All tools for cutting and carving wooden puppets. Table vice and electric sander for holding and shaping wooden puppets. Small screw eyes for string attachments in wooden marionettes. Wing nuts and bolts for portable theatres. Nails, screws and washers for marionette control bars.

Timber merchants (Lumber yards)
Soft wood for puppet bodies and limbs. Lime or fruit wood for puppet heads and hands.

Woolworth
Cup hooks for marionette control bars, neck joints and waist joints. Simple electrical fittings for puppet theatres. Simple curtain fittings for puppet theatres.

Chemists shops (Drug stores)
Paper handkerchiefs and paper towelling for papier mâché. Plaster of paris for plaster casting. *Vaseline* for lining plaster moulds. Roller bandaging for building cores for directly-modelled puppets.

Sports shops
Nylon fishing twine for marionette stringing. Table tennis balls for juggler puppets.

Useful waste materials
Remnants of cloth, fur and lambswool for puppets' clothing and hair. Used blanket material for substance beneath clothing. Newspaper for papier mâché. Old leather gloves for leather hinge joints. Springs from used ball point pens and cigarette lighters for mechanism of special movements. Used sheets for backcloth scenery and cloth puppets.

Plastic modelling substances
MOD-ROC (A Reeves product)
Reeves and Sons Limited, Lincoln Road, Enfield, Middlesex (supply in bulk to schools through education authorities)

Clifford Milburn Limited, 54 Fleet Street, London EC 4 *and* 13 Charing Cross Road, London WC 1

Alec Tiranti Limited, 72 Charlotte Street, London W 1

Also obtainable from local art shops and departmental stores

PARISCRAFT (A Johnson and Johnson product, USA)

Stage lighting
Equipment catalogues can be ordered from the following firms
Strand Electric and Engineering Company Limited, 29 King Street, London WC 2

W. J. Furse and Company Limited, 9 Cartaret Street, London SW 1

For wholesale ordering of materials in England the catalogues of the following suppliers will be found helpful

Dryad Handicrafts Limited, Northgates, Leicester

Nottingham Handicrafts Company, Helton Road, West Bridgeford, Nottingham

Atlas Handicrafts, High Street, Manchester 4

Reeves and Sons Limited, Lincoln Road, Enfield, Middlesex

Margros Limited, Monument House, Monument Way West, Woking, Surrey